The Diamond Book:

A Practical Guide
for Successful Investing

The Diamond Book:
A Practical Guide
for Successful Investing

by
Michael Freedman

Edited with
Steven Beckner

DJ-I **DOW JONES-IRWIN** Homewood, Illinois 60430

*From a Declaration of Principles jointly adopted by a Committee
of the American Bar Association and a Committee of Publishers.*

ISBN 0-87094-2234
Library of Congress Catalog Card No.80-70145
Printed in the United States of America

1234567890D76543210

To Francesca —
        my companion, lover, and wife

A Word About the Author

Michael Freedman enjoys an international reputation as one of the world's foremost authorities on investing in diamonds. He is president of Gemstone Trading Corporation, one of the oldest and largest investment diamond firms in the United States, with offices in New York, London, Antwerp, Buenos Aires and Caracas.

Mr. Freedman is editor of *The Gemletter,* a quarterly newsletter devoted to diamond market news and trends. He is a frequently featured speaker at major investment conferences throughout the nation and abroad. He writes a bi-monthly column on diamonds for *Money Maker*, the personal investment magazine published by Consumers Digest, Inc. His viewpoints and perceptions about diamond market developments are regularly sought and noted by the nation's most important business and financial publications, including: *The Wall Street Journal,* The *New York Times*, *Barron's*, *Business Week*, *Newsweek* and *Time*, among others.

Mr. Freedman's personal lifestyle and interests closely mirror his business and economic philosophy. An early convert to the "hard money" field, he began investing in gold and silver in the early seventies, before it was fashionable. After much research, he came to the conclusion that the premier hedge against inflation, currency debasement and political uncertainty was the diamond.

Mr. Freedman's research led him to Antwerp, Belgium, the world center for polished diamonds. There, he studied under one of Antwerp's leading *diamantaires* to learn the intricacies of the diamond world. Upon his return to the United States, he established Gemstone Trading Corporation, one of the first diamond investment companies. Today, Gemstone is regarded as the "granddaddy" of this young, vibrant and evolving industry, and without a doubt, Michael Freedman must be considered one of its pioneers, and most prominent spokesman.

   As a special service, Gemstone is pleased to make available their 16-page brochure entitled "What You Should Know About Diamonds Before You Invest." You can get it by sending your name and address to Gemstone Trading Corporation, Dept G, 30 Rockefeller Plaza, New York, NY 10124. Or call toll-free (800) 223-0490. New York residents call (212) 975-0777.

Preface

Investing in diamonds can be extremely profitable. Yet, for the beginner, there are the risks of making costly miscalculations.

Diamonds *are* different. Investing in them will probably be a totally new experience for you. And unless you've invested in art, antiques, stamps, etc., buying diamonds will take a little getting used to. Investing in "things" is spreading throughout America. Diamonds, like most tangibles, have many unique qualities. And it's these "unique properties" that make them an excellent investment for the 80s, and also should cause the investor to tread cautiously. It's essential to know who should and who shouldn't buy diamonds, what the liquidity factors are, and how to tell an investment grade stone from a jewelry grade diamond. No two diamonds are alike. They're not a uniform commodity like gold.

What this means is that the diamond investor must be a cautious, informed investor, who is very particular about what he buys and from whom he buys.

As in any area where subjectivity, specialized knowledge, and high stakes are involved, diamonds have been plagued by misinformation, confusion, and outright fraud. The birth of the investment diamond industry has been tumultuous. Many unscrupulous diamond companies have been preying on the public in recent years as diamonds have become an increasingly popular investment vehicle.

In this book, I explain how you can distinguish between the genuine professionals and the crooks, or just plain amateurish profiteers. There are steps you can take, and techniques you can use to protect yourself and make a sound investment in diamonds.

I'll try to demystify diamonds. As diamonds have come into greater demand as an investment, the old walls of secrecy and enigma surrounding the elusive diamond world are beginning to crumble. Widely recognized standards of scientific identification analysis and grading have been developed. It's becoming possible for the layman to identify diamonds without having to become an expert on the one hand, or, on the other, to place himself totally in the hands of someone else.

I hope the appendix and glossary will be useful for the new diamond buyer. I've tried to establish guidelines to follow so you can avoid expensive mistakes. There are many new terms that have been defined in language understandable to the layman.

There are substantial opportunities for making handsome profits in the growing area of diamond investing. Careful study and caution should enable the first-time buyer to enter the field with confidence and safety.

Table of Contents

List of Figures

The Diamond Book:
A Practical Guide
for Successful Investing

Introduction

NEW INVESTMENT STRATEGIES FOR THE 80s

Attitudes about investing have changed. The primacy of equity investing, and the safety of debt instruments, both public and private, are now being seriously questioned. Alternative investments, primarily tangibles, are being examined closely. There's a new set of rules, a new body of do's and don't's that go along with the changing investment climate.

There has been a fundamental change in the American economic climate over the last decade and a half. A virulent, highly resistant strain of double digit inflation has emerged. Economists see it persisting through the 1980s. The dollar has been devalued twice in the last decade. Government spending continues to reach record levels every year and shows no sign of abatement. The banking system is showing severe strains, and debt instruments at all levels of government are viewed with increasing skepticism. Meanwhile, OPEC is producing the most massive transfer of wealth in the history of the world.

In the light of these phenomena, most basic economic assumptions on which investment decisions are made must be re-examined.

By the end of the decade of the 70s, it had become clear that only real assets, things that had inherent value in and of themselves, could afford true protection against inflation and future economic uncertainties. Thus gold rose from $35 to $875 per ounce, and silver from $1.29 to almost $50 an ounce.

1

But if gold captured most of the attention, diamonds have captured the greatest appreciation.

During the 1970s, the prices of one carat, top-quality diamonds have risen by an average of nearly 30 percent per year! And from 1975 to early 1980, prices have risen even more spectacularly, by over 35 percent per year! The best one-carat diamond sold for around $2,000 in 1970. In early 1980, the same stone sold for over $60,000, an appreciation of some 2,000 percent. There is no single investment that I know of that would have shown a greater return on your money in the past ten years than diamonds.

Meanwhile, traditional investments were faring considerably less favorably. Over the past decade, orthodox investments failed badly to keep up with inflation. Observed *Business Week* in August 1979, "The Dow Jones Industrial average set an all-time high of 1051 in 1973, but since has sunk to its current 830. And if the Dow is adjusted for inflation, as it should be, the results are truly horrendous, an approximate loss of 50 percent in purchasing power."

The search for a real, after-inflation return on investment is growing more desperate all the time. Some investment experts suggest the primary investment strategy for the next five or ten years should be preservation of capital, more so than capital gains. Those who can preserve wealth in the difficult decade of the 80s may be the ones who will come out ahead.

Prudent American investors are starting to emulate their European counterparts. There, a centuries-old mistrust of governments has inculcated an instinct to hold a substantial portion of wealth in tangible assets. Prominent among these assets has been the diamond.

INVESTING IN DIAMONDS: AN IDEA WHOSE TIME HAS COME

To most Americans, the concept of buying diamonds for investment is rather novel. Unlike Europeans, who have known the value of diamonds for centuries, we Americans traditionally regarded diamonds as little more than a frivolous bauble, rather than the incredibly valuable, extremely rare asset they are.

Until ten years ago, virtually all diamonds sold in America were used for engagement rings and jewelry, but that picture is gradually changing. As inflation steadily worsens, and the dollar sinks lower in foreign exchange markets, the often spectacular rates of appreciation of investment grade diamonds have begun to attract the attention of investors and institutions alike.

American investors are just now beginning to wake up to the potential of diamonds. Experts estimate that over $500 million was invested in diamonds in 1979. And, while few figures are available for earlier years, I safely estimate that no more than $50 million was spent on diamond investments in 1975.

Diamonds are now being examined seriously by the professional investment community. Look at some of these recent developments.

At least 15 banks will now accept and hold diamonds as part of a Keogh or IRA program. Three years ago, not one bank in the country would offer that service. At least three of the top New York Stock Exchange brokerage houses have considered offering diamonds to their clients. Many regional brokerage firms already do so. A number of firms are looking into a diamond mutual fund, or limited partnership. I expect to see the first one launched by the end of 1980. At least two banks have offered depositors diamonds in lieu of interest. The "Prudent Man" rule under Employee Retirement Income Security Act (*ERISA*) was recently broadened so that diamonds can now be included in pension and profit programs. In-depth, feature articles on diamonds have appeared in almost every major financial newspaper and magazine during the last 12 months.

The signs are clear and unmistakable: diamonds have arrived

on the investment scene, and are taking hold as a viable alternative for the beleagured investing public entering the potentially turbulent decade of the 1980s.

ADVANTAGES OF DIAMONDS

There is good reason to believe that diamonds will do much better than merely preserve your wealth. Using the price record of the past decade as a guide, diamonds should outdistance inflation and dollar devaluation sufficiently to give you a very respectable real return on your money.

The case for adding diamonds to your portfolio is compelling, and advantages to the investor are many. Looking at just appreciation figures, the recent price trends of diamonds are impressive. And, the decade of the 80s shows even greater promise for diamonds. Diminishing supplies, rapidly increasing demand, and increasing economic, social, and political tensions around the world will probably push diamond prices up even faster in the coming decade.

These remarkable growth figures have been achieved with almost no downward price adjustments. With a few exceptions, diamond prices haven't dropped significantly since World War II. That's because diamonds enjoy the most successful price-supporting mechanism ever seen in human history — the famous DeBeers cartel.

DeBeers Consolidated Mines, a publicly traded company, incorporated in South Africa, together with its sister company, Anglo American Mining, are probably the largest and most powerful mining conglomerate in the world. With operations on every continent on the globe, DeBeers and Anglo American have huge interests in precious metals and diamonds. DeBeers controls 85 percent of the world's supply of rough (uncut) diamonds. They are committed to stabilizing and maintaining diamond price levels, and prices have had a continuous, almost unbroken, upward movement for the last 30 years.

The cartel yields another benefit for the owner of diamonds — worry free management. The basic strategy is buy and hold. Because there is so little volatility in prices, the diamond investor doesn't have to calculate the best time to buy or sell. Diamonds provide a welcome relief for investors hard hit by the roller coaster ups and downs of the commodity markets.

Another attractive feature unique to diamonds is its portability. Diamonds are the most concentrated form of wealth known to mankind. An ounce of one-carat, gem quality diamonds is worth well over $8 million, and would fit in a matchbox. Stories are legend of families whose lives or fortunes were saved by the timely conversion of assets in diamonds. Easily concealable, they can slip across international boundaries safely — they don't set off airport metal detectors. And unlike gold, there is no instance that I know of in which governments confiscated diamonds by making it illegal to own them. (Gold, of course, has been confiscated innumerable times by various governments, including our own in 1933.)

In fact, there are no regulations on owning diamonds. Buying a diamond is a private discreet transaction. Currently, there are no reporting requirements. In a sense, diamonds can be thought of as bearer bonds.

Liquidity, a factor that should also be considered before buying diamonds, is improving every year. While diamonds don't have the "instant liquidity" of the stock or commodity exchanges, they are surprisingly liquid. With the exception of the precious metals, diamonds probably have a higher degree of liquidity than any other "tangible." And as more investors and institutions enter the field, the diamond market will become increasingly easy to enter and exit.

As for the supply/demand equation on diamonds, that too is bullish. Supplies are level, and demand is increasing. World

6

production for gem quality rough diamonds has been level for the past three years at around 10 million carats (in spite of strong demand). A few new mines have been discovered, primarily in Botswana, and there are recent, but unproven discoveries in Australia, but, in a report published a few years ago, the Smithsonian Institute estimated there were no more than 30 to 40 years worth of diamond reserves in the ground at current rates of consumption. Demand, on the other hand, has been increasing tremendously, and shows no signs of abating.

Investing in diamonds is not simple, but not as complicated as it may seem. Many people are overawed by the seeming complexities of the diamond industry. This book attempts to remove the complexities and provide a simple perspective which should enable you to feel confident and secure when making an investment in diamonds.

1

The Romance of Diamonds

From Biblical times up through the Marilyn Monroe and Elizabeth Taylor era, diamonds have had a long, romantic, often exciting history.

Even before the science of cutting and polishing the world's hardest substance was developed, diamonds were cherished. Discovered in India's Golcanda region sometime in the first millenium before Christ, rough (uncut) diamonds were highly valued and comprised a large portion of the treasure chests of potentates and maharajahs.

In fact, to this day, some of the world's great gem collections are located in that ancient country, although most of them have now been liquidated. Recently, what was described by the press as "a small portion" of the last Nizam of Hyderabad's gem collection went on the auction block. Opening bid — over $25 million. The potentate's collection — accumulated over many generations — was said to be so vast that precious stones, including emeralds and rubies as well as diamonds, were left to lie about the cellar floor of the Nizam's palace. The largest item of the collection — a 184-carat stone called "Jacob's Diamond," which the Indian government has declared a national treasure — was reportedly used by the prince as a paperweight, wrapped in newspapers and left openly on his desk.

The Indians thought that diamonds grew in the ground like the seeds of a plant. They weighed and valued diamonds in relation to the seeds of the carob tree, which were thought to be a

uniform unit of measurement. The carob seed evolved into the
"carat," the unit in which diamonds are still weighed today.
(One carat equals 1/142 of an ounce or 1/5 gram.) Some of the
world's biggest and most famous diamonds "grew" and were
harvested in the alluvial deposits of India. Among these were
the fabled "Hope" and "Koh-i-noor," as well as the "Orloff,"
"Great Mogul" and "Shah."

A steady flow of diamonds came from India, from ancient
times through the eighteenth century. Diamonds found their
way all over the known, civilized world before Christ. They are
mentioned in the Bible and other ancient texts. The Greeks
knew diamonds, having given us the root of the word: *adamas*,
which means unyielding or unbreakable. Pliny the Elder, the
Roman philosopher who lived and wrote in the first century
A.D., wrote of a secret "Valley of Diamonds, " where he said
congealed bolts of lightning were recovered from the earth.

Wherever diamonds made their way, they became centers of
mystery, intrigue and superstition. As its name suggest, diamonds have always symbolized the ultimate in strength.
Napoleon, who once used a diamond as collateral for a bank
loan, also had a diamond set in the hilt of his sword.

From time immemorial, diamonds have had attributed to
them characteristics ranging from the power to protect and to
cure to an ability to bring death and misfortune. Diamonds
were, on one hand, thought to cure wounds in ancient Greece
and Rome. But, on the other hand, there have been legends
about particular diamonds' destructive capabilities.

Most famous for this is the Hope Diamond. Now residing in
the Smithsonian Institution's fabulous gem collection in Washington, the Hope has been associated with a continuous history
of death and misfortune. From Louis XIV of France through
recent times, strange circumstances have befallen its owners.

We all know the fate of Marie Antoinette, among whose
alleged extravagant peccadilloes that hastened the French Rev-

olution was the acquisition of an expensive diamond necklace. At any rate, after she was beheaded by the Jacobins, the deep blue Hope diamond was stolen, recut to its present size of 44.50 carats to escape detection, and then disappeared for several decades.

In 1830, it reappeared in London, where it became the property of Thomas Hope. Later it was the property of the Sultan of Turkey — until revolution forced him too to get rid of the diamond. Sold in Paris in 1908, for the then astounding sum of $400,000, it was acquired by Mrs. Evalyn Walsh McLean. She wore it as a pendant when she wasn't hiding it nervously in the cushions of an armchair, as the story goes. In 1958, Harry Winston, the famous New York jeweler donated the stone, whose value is now considered incalculable, to the Smithsonian for all citizens to enjoy. And many say our country has not been the same since.

Then there is the Koh-i-noor. When Prince Shah Shuja of Afghanistan owned the massive, 186-carat stone, legend has it that he was tormented by temporary blindness and pain for several days until he finally got rid of it. The Koh-i-noor is now among the crown jewels of the Queen of England.

Diamonds, of course, have always been associated with royalty. And, in fact, they have and continue to play an important role in national treasuries. Queen Isabella of Spain's jewelry helped finance Christopher Columbus' voyage of discovery to America. Even today, jewels are amassed in such countries as the Phillipines and Iran.

The once jewel-bedecked Shah of Iran fled the country in the wake of the revolution in early 1979 with a good supply of fine quality diamonds. But the prizes of his family's dynastic diamond holdings remain in Teheran, where they lie in the national treasury and continue to back the rial, the Iranian currency. Even more recently, we had the curious case of (now deposed) "Emperor" Jean-Bedel Bokassa of the Central African Republic and his alleged diamond bribes to French President Valery Giscard d'Estaing.

Because of their great concentration of wealth in a small space and their resultant portability, diamonds have, for centuries been the "best friend" of fugitives and refugees — not merely for Shahs and Emperors. There have been many cases where large numbers of ordinary citizens have resorted to diamonds as a way of bribing their way to freedom and as a method of financing a new life once they secured their freedom.

If it seems that the diamond industry is dominated by Jewish people, it is for a very good reason. For centuries Jews have been a persecuted people. They could only be involved in businesses that allowed them great mobility. Diamonds were ideally suited to this requirement, and Jewish people naturally gravitated to the industry. Then too, Jews were often prohibited from owning land or participating in other fields of endeavor.

Many Jews who had fled from the Spanish Inquisition or from later persecutions, having converted their shops, land and other assets into diamonds, stayed in the diamond trade when they relocated in Northern Europe. Gradually, a Jewish-dominated diamond industry arose in such places as Antwerp and Amsterdam. And although they were excluded by the Renaissance-era guild system, the Jews made the diamond trade evolve and prosper. Passing their experience and expertise from generation to generation, the art of diamond cutting and trading customs began to develop into the sophisticated, though sometimes enigmatic, industry we know today.

But certainly Jews are not the only people to have discovered the usefulness of diamonds. People of many races and nationalities have found themselves threatened during times of war and economic chaos and have resorted to diamonds. Even today, there are refugees from the turmoil of Southeast Asia who owe their lives, freedom, and prosperity to a few strategically hidden precious stones. It is no coincidence that one of the most rapidly growing markets for diamonds today is in Asia.

During World War II, it was reported that agents of the OSS were often sent behind German Lines with diamonds. There was no need to carry counterfeit currency or much weightier gold when a diamond could be converted to cash or be used to barter for information or for survival itself.

The history of diamonds is filled with delightful anecdotes and stories. It is a centuries-old tale, and new chapters are added daily.

2

The History of Diamonds: From Volcanic Origins to the Formation of DeBeers

THE DIAMOND: ITS NATURE, SOURCE, AND HISTORY OF ITS PRODUCTION

The mystery and romance of diamonds, while interesting, are less important to the investor than an understanding of some of the critical elements of minerology, mining, and distribution of diamonds, for these elements greatly influence rarity and therefore the value of diamonds.

Just what is this substance called diamond? What are the factors of geology, mining, cutting, and the other facets of bringing an individual stone to market that make the diamond so rare and so prized?

Ironic as it sounds, a diamond is nothing more than carbon, one of the most common elements known to man. A diamond is no different chemically from the charcoal you barbecue a steak over, or the graphite in the pencil you write with, or the coal that heats your home and factory. The difference is that the carbon in a diamond has been subjected to tremendous heat and pressure until it has been compressed into an extremely hard, crystalline form.

FORMATION OF DIAMONDS

Diamonds were formed eons ago, many miles below the

13

earth's crust, in the unstable layer known as the "mantle." There, shifting layers of rock subjected carbon deposits to temperatures of several thousand degrees Fahrenheit and to millions of pounds of pressure per square inch. Under these forces, carbon (sometimes with slight impurities of nitrogen and an assortment of other elements) was restructured into the hardest possible configuration — a crystal cube.

Diamonds were then brought to the surface through volcanic activity — the molten magma turning to hardened lava flows and leaving what are known as "kimberlite pipes," named after the town in South Africa where the biggest discovery of modern times was made. These "pipes," like long pieces of tubing, are really the upward channels, or vents, of old volcanoes that brought the diamond-bearing liquid ore close to the earth's surface.

Later, a combination of geological upheavals or "faulting" of the planet's crust and erosion exposed these "pipes." The action of wind and water gradually removed the softer rock and loosened the diamond crystals embedded within. Many of the diamonds were then washed downstream, as far as the sea in many cases. They were dropped off in gravel beds and then often buried once more under tons of sand.

The first diamonds were discovered far removed from their volcanic origins, along rivers and seacoasts. Indeed, many are still found there. But as man's unquenchable desire for the white rocks persisted and grew, he began to trace them back to their source, so that today there are deep, highly capitalized, sub-surface excavations of diamond-bearing pipes.

The fact that diamonds have survived so much geological tumult, while all around them such rugged substances as granite were eroding into dust, is testament to their hardness. On Moh's hardness scale of one to ten, diamond is regarded as a ten, with such precious stones as ruby and sapphire (forms of corundum) listed as nine. But that is not an adequate indication of the hardness of the diamond. A more scientific reading reveals that a diamond is 140 times harder than sapphire and ruby, its nearest competitors. A diamond will scratch any other substance known to man. The only substance that can scratch a diamond is another diamond.

Among its other important characteristics, a diamond has a specific gravity of 3.52 and a refractive index of 2.42. Both of these distinguishing features can be used by a competent lab technician to tell the difference between a diamond and other minerals or artificial diamonds.

Specific gravity simply means, for our purposes, the relative heaviness of a substance. Diamonds are much lighter than zircons and other diamond substitutes. Actual synthetic diamonds with the same characteristics as a real diamond can be made and are made in large quantities for industrial uses, but it is very difficult and therefore not profitable to make them in gem quality.

The refractive index, which is a measure of a stone's ability to bend light passing through it, is also distinctive for diamonds. A diamond's ability to gather and bend light and, given a well-proportioned cut, return the light to the viewer with minimum loss of brilliance, is what gives the diamond its famous "fire." No other stone, real or fake, has the same ability.

EARLY DIAMOND MINING

As mentioned earlier, diamonds were first mined on a large and continuous scale in India. And diamonds were dug in that country from their discovery hundreds of years before the birth of Christ through the early part of the 1700s before diminishing into insignificance. Then, in 1725, diamonds were discovered in the jungles of Brazil. Here, as in India, diamonds were (and continue to be) uncovered in so-called "alluvial deposits," that is in old and existing riverbeds. It took a while for Brazilian diamonds to win acceptance, although they were of excellent quality, because initially people regarded India as *the* source of diamonds.

But soon all of this was to pale into insignificance. Brazil's preeminence in diamond production lasted until 1866, when diamonds were discovered in South Africa. History records that one Erasmus Stephanus Jacobs, young son of a tenant farmer near the northern Cape Colony settlement of Hopetown, was playing with pebbles with some other children, when a particularly bright stone caught his eye. The owner of the "DeKalk" farm, Schalk Van Niekerk, came into possession of the stone. And he, in turn, put it in the hands of a skeptical, but curious trader named John O'Reilly. Much to O'Reilly's surprise, inspection by minerologists revealed that, in fact, it was a diamond, weighing more than 21 carats. He accepted the then quite respectable sum of 500 pounds sterling for it.

As word spread of the discovery, the beginnings of a diamond rush developed. Slowly at first, people began prospecting along rivers in the region. And other discoveries were made. But skepticism remained the rule for a while, especially outside South Africa. London minerologist J.R. Gregory ventured to South Africa to see for himself and returned to report disdainfully in an 1868 issue of *Geological Magazine*:

> . . . I made a very lengthy examination of the districts where diamonds are said to have been found, but saw no indication that would suggest the finding of diamonds or diamond-bearing deposits in any of these localities. The geological character of that part of the country renders it impossible . . . that they could have been discovered there . . . It seems conclusive to me that the whole story of the Cape diamond discovery is false . . . and is simply one of many schemes for trying to promote the employment and expenditure of capital in searching for this precious substance in the colony.

Gregory and others pronounced the O'Reilly and other South African diamonds to be, in fact, Brazilian.

But it wasn't long before even bigger discoveries made any South African self-promotion efforts quite unnecessary. For in March 1869, a black shepherd, Booi by name, was tending goats near the Orange River, when he happened across a beautiful, bluish-white diamond weighing 83 1/2 carats. He was steered to the same Mr. Van Niekerk, whose farm had yielded South Africa's first diamond. The Dutch farmer was very happy to buy it from the native for the price of 500 sheep, 11 cattle, one horse, a saddle and bridle, and a gun — altogether worth about $2,000. Van Niekerk lost no time selling the stone for $60,000. "The Star of Africa," as it soon came to be known, was sent to England, cut and resold to the Earl of Dudley for $125,000.

Word of the magnificent discovery and the princely sum it had brought now attracted prospectors by the thousands. They came from as far away as the gold fields of California and the "outback" of Australia. Camping in tent towns with their families, hordes of "star"-struck prospectors dug, panned and otherwise searched for diamonds along the Orange and Vaal Rivers.

Soon, however, even this diamond rush was surpassed — and totally altered — as interest shifted to so-called "dry diggings." Towering above the banks of the Vaal was a hill known as the "Colesberg Koppie." That hill no longer exists. What remains is one of the widest, deepest, man-made holes in the world. For on the crest of that hill, which was actually the upper extrusion of an ancient volcanic fissure, so many diamonds were found in 1870 that river diggings became like cold leftovers for serious miners. Thousands more rushed into South Africa, and the small (less than 15 acres) area of Colesberg Koppie was covered with a swarm of hungry prospectors, each digging away on claims of 30 square feet and less. In practically no time, the hill vanished, and a gaping hole filled with nearly 2,000 claims developed, going deeper and deeper beneath the surface.

EARLY FOUNDATION OF DE BEERS

In the immediate area of Colesberg Koppie, which became known as "New Rush, " there were several other mines, the richest centering on the farm of G.A. DeBeers. Altogether it is estimated that over 20,000 prospectors and their families were encamped in the Vaal River area, with close to 4,000 claims staked out.

Not surprisingly, unimaginable chaos (legally and logistically) ensued. Gradually, however, claims were consolidated. Leaders of the merger trend were two very different men: Barney Barnato, a former boxer, actor and circus performer of humble East London beginnings, and Cecil John Rhodes, the cultured, scholarly son of an English minister. While Barnato bought up claims to the Kimberly Mine, Rhodes bought up the DeBeers Mine. In 1880, one stood as the head of the Barnato Diamond Company and the other of the DeBeers Mining Company, two very large concerns for their day.

But Rhodes, the aspiring empire builder, who had been elected to the Cape Parliament while still in his twenties, would not be satisfied with less than total domination of the diamond industry. With the financial help of the House of Rothschild, the Oxford graduate set out to buy up all rival claims in the Kimberly Mine. This culminated in 1888, when Rhodes succeeded in gaining control of a majority of the shares of the Kimberly central company. Barnato and other constituents of that company agreed to become "governors" of Rhodes' combined company, DeBeers Consolidated Mines Limited. This new company bought the total assets of the old company for £ 5,338,650 ($26 million), issuing the largest check that had ever been written up to that time.

DeBeers Consolidated Mines then proceeded, under Rhodes' visionary leadership, not only to explore the length and breadth of South Africa for diamonds, but also to finance the British South Africa Company, which, with the help of the British army, colonized Rhodesia and most of central Africa.

In 1904, another fabulous new mine was found further north in the Transvaal, near the present sites of Johannesburg and Pretoria. And in the following year, the biggest diamond ever discovered — the 3,106-carat "Cullinan" — was found. The fist-sized rock was cut into the 530-carat Cullinan I, the 317-carat Cullinan II, as well as nearly 100 smaller stones. Once more, DeBeers had to struggle to maintain its domination.

DE BEERS AND ANGLO-AMERICAN JOIN FORCES

Cecil Rhodes died in 1902, but what he started, another unique character, also English, inherited and expanded. Ernest Oppenheimer, who started in the diamond business in London while still a teenager, carved out his own chapter in the annals of industrial empire building. With the American financial backing of J.P. Morgan, Oppenheimer and his Anglo-American Corporation, established in 1917, set out in the 1920s to challenge DeBeers.

The key was getting an exclusive concession over the rich diamond deposits along the coast of South-West Africa (Namibia). There, where the Kama desert meets the Atlantic Ocean, the Buffels and Orange Rivers had carried millions of carats of fine gems from their inland pipe sources. By the mid-twenties, the alluvial deposits stretching along the coast north of Alexander Bay into the former German colony had become the biggest single source of diamonds.

With control of these deposits, which even today yield an estimated 95 percent gem quality stones, Oppenheimer did not find it overly difficult to come to terms with DeBeers. In 1929, he became chairman of the board of DeBeers Consolidated Mines. In 1930, the Oppenheimer-controlled Consolidated Diamond Mines of Southwest Africa merged with DeBeers. Anglo-American and DeBeers exchanged stock, so that today each company holds interests in the other. The Oppenheimer family still controls the Anglo-American Group, which includes gold and other mining interests all over the world.

Oppenheimer too had a vision. It was to take what Rhodes had started and build it into the most effective cartel the world had ever known, effectively controlling the prices of worldwide diamond output. He was, of course, notoriously successful in doing just that, and doing it to such an extent that DeBeers' domination, now under the direction of his son Harry, remains virtually unchallenged to this day. In fact, as we shall see, while there is speculation about slippage in the control of DeBeers, there is good reason to believe that, in some respects, DeBeers is becoming even more powerful.

3

Diamond Production, Supply and Demand in the Modern Era

Present day South Africa has inherited what Barney Barnato, Cecil Rhodes, and Ernest Oppenheimer built. Today that nation remains at the top of the diamond-producing heap — with DeBeers calling the shots.

Despite inroads by mines in other countries, South Africa is still the single biggest producer of gem quality diamonds.

With 11 DeBeers-controlled mines in production, South Africa provided 3,435,000 carats or about 31 percent of the world's total gemstone production of 10,867,000 carats in 1975, according to the U.S. Bureau of Mining Statistics. However, 1975 was a low production year. Production has been as high as 13,297,000 carats (in 1970), according to the same source. (See **Figure 1**). And in his prestigious "Executive Report on Investment Diamonds," published by *Precious Stones Newsletter*, Jean-Francois Moyersoen predicted annual gem diamond production will rise to over 15 million ounces in 1980, and to as high as 16 million by 1985— before dropping off sharply once more.

In terms of "normal" production levels, South Africa probably contributes more like 26 percent of gem production. That's still good enough for number one status, but a far cry

Figure 1.
Rough Diamond Production (Thousand Carats)

COUNTRY	1977			1978P			1979e		
	Gem	Indus-trial	Total	Gem	Indus-trial	Total	Gem	Indus-trial	Total
Africa:									
Angola	265	88	353	525	175	700	562	188	750
Botswana	404	2,287	2,691	418	2,367	2,785	500	2,840	3,340
Central African Empire	178	119	297	199	85	284	210	90	300
Ghana e	230	1,717	1,947	142	1,281	1,423	150	1,350	1,500
Guinea e	25	55	80	25	55	80	27	58	85
Ivory Coast	7	11	18	—	10	10	5	5	5
Lesotho	7	35	42	13	53	66	14	56	70
Liberia	163	163	326	128	180	308	130	180	310
Sierra Leone	423	538	961	283	424	707	285	425	710
South Africa, Republic of:									
Premier mine	502	1,508	2,010	496	1,487	1,983	495	1,485	1,980
Other DeBeers properties	2,796	2,287	5,083	2,903	2,376	5,279	2,900	2,300	5,200
Other	330	220	550	278	186	464	275	185	460
Total	3,628	4,015	7,643	3,678	4,049	7,727	3,670	3,970	7,640
South-West Africa, Territory of: (Namibia)	1,901	100	2,001	1,803	95	1,898	1,850	100	1,950
Tanzania	204	204	408	146	147	293	145	145	290
Zaire	561	10,652	11,213	562	10,688	11,250	560	10,600	11,160
Other areas:									
Brazil	33	32	65	43	43	86	45	45	90
Guyana	7	10	17	7	10	17	7	10	17
India	15	3	18	14	2	16	14	2	16
Indonesia e	3	12	15	3	12	15	3	12	15
U.S.S.R. e	2,100	8,200	10,300	2,150	8,400	10,550	2,200	8,500	10,700
Venezuela	204	483	687	278	460	738	285	465	750
WORLD TOTAL	10,358	28,724	39,082	10,417	28,536	38,953	10,657	29,041	39,698

eEstimate.   PPreliminary.   Source: U.S. Bureau of Mines

from the old days in the early part of the century when South
Africa produced close to three-quarters.

Actually, in terms of total diamond production, including
industrial diamonds, South Africa is only third, behind Zaire
and the Soviet Union. But low quality stones make up the bulk
of those two nations' output. Total production averages 40-45
million carats worldwide each year. But since this book is primarily concerned with investment diamonds, that figure will
not be terribly meaningful for us. The important thing to
remember is that only about one-fourth, at most, of the total
yearly diamond production is of gem quality. But of that, say,
10 million carats of "gems," only an estimated 15 percent is in
the range of quality that is advisable for the investor to consider. (See **Figure 2**).

Figure 2.
The Diamond Production Spectrum

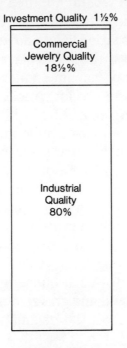

Investment Quality 1½%

Commercial
Jewelry Quality
18½%

Industrial
Quality
80%

Outside of South Africa proper the most important source of gems is the South African-controlled territory of South-West Africa, the aspiring independent nation of Namibia. It is along the beaches in the southern part of South-West Africa that DeBeers operates its most lucrative mining venture, Ernest Oppenheimer's original Consolidated Diamond Mines (CDM). It's actually a surface mining operation, stretching along over 60 miles of desert shoreline — and even out into the ocean itself. A similar coastal venture is in the Namaqualand area of South Africa's own shoreline. Over 95 percent of the stones that are recovered there are of gem quality. Over 1.6 million carats are recovered there annually, good enough to claim over 13 percent of total world gem production.

To harvest these stones, giant earthmoving equipment burrows down through as much as 80 feet of sand in order to expose underlying gravel beds. Lately, CDM has even taken to building giant sea walls several hundred yards offshore, draining the area within and excavating for diamonds there. Tons and tons of diamond-bearing sand and gravel are then trucked to plants where careful sifting takes place and where, under the latest methods, an X-ray machine, guided by the fluorescence of diamonds, detects the precious rocks amid the rubble and signals air jets to eject them. Meanwhile, hundreds of black workmen, who live in company compounds and work under the tightest security imaginable, carefully comb each crack and crevice in the exposed rock floor of the beach and ocean, searching for carats that were left behind.

According to a report from CDM, slightly over 13 carats of diamond are recovered out of every 100 metric tons of material processed. This is down from nearly 15 carats per 100 metric tons in the sixties, showing that even this rich source is depleting. Put another way, for each ounce of diamond recovered, 175 million ounces of sand and gravel must be treated. Not surprisingly, given worldwide inflation and the greater difficulty in extricating the remaining stones, the cost per carat of recovering diamonds from coastal deposits has risen from $14 in 1969 to $40 today, according to the "Executive Report."

Although less safe for the miners, sub-surface mining actually presents better statistics. The Premier Mine, for instance, yields some 30 carats per 100 metric tons of kimberlite pipe that is excavated and processed. The cost is also, generally, somewhat lower. But, the difference is that only a third, at most, of the stones that are discovered are of gem quality. Incidentally, a vast new reserve of diamonds was recently discovered beneath the old Premier Mine, and that is now being exploited. It's called the Pretoria Mine.

Despite this new source, South African production can be expected to continue to diminish as existing deposits are gradually stripped of better grade stones. This raises concern about future supplies, because it will force diamond buyers to depend more heavily on the rest of Africa and other parts of the world.

MINES OUTSIDE OF SOUTH AFRICA

With South-West Africa (Namibia) the single most lucrative source of gem quality stones, the struggle of the Marxist SWAPO guerrillas to take over that South-Africa-Controlled territory is a real threat. Annual production from South-West Africa has been worth $400 million, returning after-tax profits of $157 million to DeBeers in 1978, or 22 percent of its total profits. A Communist Namibia could probably be expected to boot DeBeers out, and while a new regime might try to continue production, it is highly doubtful that it could do so as efficiently as DeBeers. The flow of stones from that source might become disrupted and erratic.

Ample precedent for such a scenario can be found in Angola.

When Soviet-supported, Marxist guerrillas led by the late Aghostino Neto took over and kicked the Portuguese out of their former colony, they also bid farewell to the "foreign capitalists" that were supplying the world, at peak in 1971, with 1.8 million carats of gem-quality diamonds. In 1975, production was less than 350,000 carats, and since 1976, production has been stilled completely. There are rumors now that production may resume from the old Diamang Company mines, with the Angolan government in partnership with DeBeers-related interests. But the doubt remains.

Other significant diamond deposits on the African continent include those in Botswana, Lesotho, Central African Republic, Sierra Leone, Tanzania, Liberia, Ghana, Ivory Coast, and Zaire. It is conceivable that any one or all of these (mostly) young and unstable nations could be subjected to spreading Communist insurrection, revolution, and expropriation of foreign capital interests.

In a number of these countries, notably Lesotho, Botswana, and Tanzania, DeBeers has a substantial interest in the ownership and management of the mines. Those who forsake DeBeers participation generally have much less efficient exploitation of their deposits.

A disturbing trend has been for the various governments to gradually ease DeBeers out of the picture. Botswana, which is expected to become a growing factor in the total world supply picture, is the most prominent example. DeBeers opened the important Orapa mine in the middle of the forbidding Kalahari Desert in late 1971. The mine was to be owned equally by DeBeers and the Botswana government, but recently the government "renegotiated," telling DeBeers that, henceforth, it will receive only 25 percent of the profits.

Other countries, most importantly Ghana and Sierra Leone, do not deal with the DeBeers cartel at all. That is, their stones bypass the DeBeers marketing mechanism in London, and are instead sold directly to cutters. That is a small negative for DeBeers' largely successful effort to control the supply coming onto the market. The more important trend — toward government expropriation of DeBeers' holdings and so forth — is probably a different matter, however.

Outside the African continent, by far the most important producer is the Soviet Union. Discovered in the early 1950s, Russian mines in the Siberian region of Yakutsk have been producing a steadily growing amount of diamonds. Estimates — and that's all they are for the secretive Soviets — range from 10 to 12 million carats, but only about a quarter of their output is of gem quality. The U.S. Bureau of Mines estimates Soviet gem production at just short of 2 million carats in 1975. Russia is thought to have some of the world's richest known kimberlite pipes, producing far more carats per 100 metric tons than the typical African mine. But the stones tend to average much smaller.

Brazil has slipped considerably from its former preeminence in diamond mining, but it still produces annually some 150,000 carats, many of which are of good size and quality. Exploration continues deep in the jungles along the Amazon River. DeBeers is involved in two mining companies and a third exploration company, in which it holds substantial portions of stock.

Perhaps the largest potential producer of the future is Australia. Although the full extent of its reserves is still unproven, substantial and very encouraging discoveries have been made in the so-called Kimberley region of Western Australia. The Ashton joint venture, led by Conzinc Riotinto of Australia and other smaller claim holders, has made some positive discoveries there. But the prospect remains uncertain.

As the *Financial Times* of London observed in mid-1979:

> The largest announced (Australian diamond) has been one of 6.47 carats, but the discovery of many more diamonds of con-

siderably larger size would be required to rate the prospect as exciting. At the moment it ranks as no more than intriguing, but these are still early days and the many kimberlite 'pipes' discovered have been barely scratched. At last report, deeper drilling samples were being taken in a number of areas.

FUTURE SUPPLIES

To summarize the overall supply picture, new diamond discoveries *are* being made, and new sources of supply *are* coming on line. However, at the same time, old sources are giving out, so that at best new sources seem to be doing little more than replacing old. Without taking into consideration the danger of politically induced supply disruptions, it appears that the Smithsonian estimate of a 30 to 40 year world supply of diamonds is accurate.

Moreover, the cost of recovering those known reserves is soaring and will continue to do so. As existing mines go deeper and deeper into the kimberlite pipe, costs rise. What's more, both the number and the size of diamonds reaches a point of diminishing returns and starts decreasing rapidly at greater depths. For instance, the "Executive Report," citing DeBeers figures, notes that in the Premier Mine, the number of carats recovered per 100 metric tons has declined from 221 at the upper levels, to 44 at the 400 meter level, to only 31.5 at the present level of 450 meters. Comparable, if less dramatic, numbers could be cited for other mines.

At the same time, the size of the diamonds discovered fell dramatically. In the period 1870-1920, a total of 1,872 diamonds of 100 carats and larger (up to 1,000 carats) were found. But in the period 1920-1970, only 705 such stones were located. Just in the last decade, the average size of diamonds has fallen off remarkably. At the Namaqualand deposits, for instance, the same source reported, the average size in 1972 was 1.03 carats, but dropped to only 0.67 carats by 1977. The cost of recovering a carat of diamonds at that particular mine went from $6 to $17 in the roughly comparable period of 1969 - 1977.

Of course, supply cannot be looked at in isolation. The equally important factor of increased demand must be considered in conjunction with it. And remember, we're talking about demand for gem diamonds generally and investment grade diamonds, in particular. When we talk of 10 million carats of gem diamonds, we are first of all talking about rough caratage. As much as half of that weight is lost in the meticulous cutting process.

But even before cutting, probably no more than 180,000 carats maximum of investment grade diamonds is brought forth in any given year. After cutting, no more than 60,000 carats of cut and polished diamonds are available to an increasingly sophisticated world of investors.

When you consider that the annual production of gem diamonds is only some 5 million carats greater now than in the World War I era, while population and purchasing power has exploded incalculably (at a different rate in different areas of the world obviously), it is not hard to see why diamond prices have soared. How much of this is due to natural scarcity and how much to DeBeers-manipulated scarcity is relatively unimportant. The effect is the same.

DEMAND RISES

But the effect of DeBeers cannot be underestimated, as we shall see in the next chapter. Not only has it steadied supply, it has enhanced demand. We in America now take it for granted that women wear diamonds. We assume it was always so. Not true. Fifty years ago, a tiny minority of married women owned diamonds. Now over 80 percent own them. This phenomenal cultural change is thanks largely to the incessant sloganeering of DeBeers: "Diamonds are forever," and so forth.

Now, the same trick is working in countries such as Japan. There in the land of the rising sun, the rising yen and the retiring female, who would have thought that diamond engagement rings would come to be an obligatory marriage custom? A mere decade ago only nine percent of Japanese women entered marriage with a diamond engagement ring. Now fully 50 percent do, and the figure is rising.

Moreover, few Americans ever heard of an "investment diamond" as recently as ten years ago? Very, very few investors — certainly in this country — bought loose diamonds for the sake of investment alone. Now, however, perhaps 20 percent of the gem quality diamonds that are bought each year are bought for that primary purpose. That figure was cited by Raoul Delveaux, Director-General of the Antwerp's presigious Diamond High Council, who made that estimate in a recent *Forbes* magazine article.

There are probably about 25,000 diamond investors in America today. Most are people with a net worth of $100,000 or more who have previously bought gold and silver out of concern about inflation, depreciation of the dollar, and other economic uncertainties. While some investors mount their diamonds, and while many purchasers of engagement rings hope for appreciation of their "investments," most truly investment grade stones are bought and kept loose.

And, as indicated earlier, worsening inflation and currency depreciation all over the world will undoubtedly increase demand even further. But even if inflation slackens, even if we plunge into another depression, diamonds have a built-in insurance policy that insulates them from the worst ravages of economic contingencies that effect other types of investments. And that's DeBeers. So, before we continue to survey the structure of the diamond industry beyond the stage of primary production, let's take a better look at the unique organization and how it functions.

4

From DeBeers to You — How the Cartel Distributes Diamonds to the Industry

You can't really understand the unique investment qualities of diamonds without understanding the function and performance of the DeBeers cartel.

It's an historical anomaly: a "monopoly" that works. No cartel, including OPEC, has ever worked as effectively as the one headed by DeBeers Consolidated Mines. To call it a monopoly — and it very nearly is the *single seller* that word implies — is only half the story. Just as importantly, it is virtually a "monopsony," which means a *single buyer*.

It became clear to Oppenheimer in 1927, that centralized control over the distribution and pricing of diamonds, both from within and without South Africa, needed to be exerted. For in 1927, as DeBeers' existing output from the Kimberley and other deposits was supplemented by heavy new flows of diamonds from the Southwest African coastal deposits and other alluvial deposits at Lichtenburg, prices of diamonds dropped.

Prices of rough stones fell an estimated 24 percent, according to Godehard Lenzon in his 1965 study *The History of Diamond Production and the Diamond Trade* (Barrie and Jenkins, Ltd., London, 1970). It was one of the few times, and one of the last times, in this country that there has been a marked decline in rough diamond prices. Diamond prices also fell in the early years of the Depression, but by learning from the 1927 experience, Oppenheimer is credited with bringing the diamond industry through the Depression intact, if not unscathed, and with the image of diamonds as an investment very much enhanced. How did he do it?

In 1930, Oppenheimer established DeBeers' most important subsidiary, the Diamond Corporation Limited. Its task was to secure agreements with as many non-DeBeers producers as possible to purchase and then market their stones. As the network of long-term producer contracts developed, up to 85 percent of the world's diamonds came to be sold by DeBeers' London-based Diamond Trading Corporation, usually known as the Central Selling Organization (CSO) — also popularly known as "the Syndicate."

Times were rough in the 1930s, as the depression that began in the United States spread worldwide. Diamond prices fell, as did all prices. But the newly in-place DeBeers cartel mechanism so tightly regulated the flow of goods to the market that, even in these years, prices were held relatively stable. Since then, the record of DeBeers-induced price escalation — on a steady, inexorable, and generally predictable basis — has endeared almost all of the world's diamond producing countries to their arrangement with DeBeers.

By virtue of its long-term purchasing and marketing contracts with almost all of the world's diamond producers, DeBeers is both the prime buyer and seller for the whole world.

Although DeBeers itself produces less than 20 percent of the world's diamonds from its mines in South Africa, South-West Africa, Botswana, and Lesotho, it controls between 80 and 85 percent of total worldwide production through the long-term contracts mentioned above. DeBeers even handles the major part of the production of the Soviet Union, although it is done more covertly now than in the past.

It would be hard to find a more financially muscular firm.

Even an oil company would be envious. The 1978 Financial Statement of DeBeers Consolidated Mines Ltd. reported income of 1.219 billion rands (about $1.47 billion at the current rate of $1.21 per rand). Aftertax profits were 750,579,000 rands ($908,200,590). Earnings per equity share were 205.5 South African cents ($2.48 per share).

Over the last decade the profit picture of DeBeers has steadily improved, increasing over six times. Return on total assets rose from 11 percent in 1970 to over 30 percent in 1978, while return on net worth rose from 14 percent to over 43 percent in the same span of years.

Naturally, everyone connected with diamonds is concerned about its financial health and any threats to the cartel.

One of the areas of concern is South-West Africa (Namibia). Those coastal deposits now contribute over 20 percent of the company's total profits. However, DeBeers is very well aware of the potential threats in Namibia. That is one of the reasons why it has moved with such deliberation to diversify its mining operations geographically. Botswana and Lesotho, which, in the long run, may be both more dependable and more profitable, are being developed rapidly and are expected to provide a greater and greater share of DeBeers rough diamonds and DeBeers profits. Further, as mentioned earlier, DeBeers has taken an interest in diamond exploration and mining in other parts of the world, including both Brazil and Australia.

It is important to remember that DeBeers is not entirely dependent on diamonds. (See **Figure 3**). It is an internationally diversified giant. Among its holdings and financial interests, usually in consort with Anglo-American (DeBeers owns 33 percent of Anglo-American, and Anglo-American owns 30 percent of DeBeers) are: Englehard Metals, Hudson Bay Mining, gold mines such as Free State Geduld, Vaal Reefs, East Rand Gold & Uranium, Rustenburg platinum, as well as holdings of portions of such Canadian companies as Francona Oil and Gas, Lytton

Figure 3.
DeBeers' Worldwide Holdings
(Numbers = % of ownership)

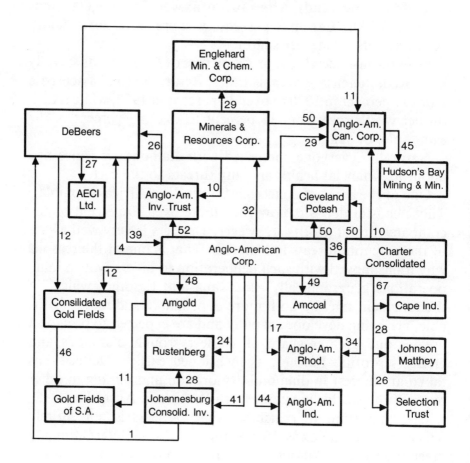

Chart, above, reflects DeBeers' direct ownership interests of other companies, and indirect ownership interests through Anglo-American Corp., a holding company which serves as parent to DeBeers. Harry F. Oppenheimer, chairman of DeBeers is also chairman of Anglo-American Corp.

Source: Andrew H. Schwartz, *The Value Line Investment Survey.*

Minerals, Tombill Mines, and a joint venture copper mine — all through its subsidiary Debhold (Canada) Limited. And that's just a partial listing.

Little wonder that some 20,000 Americans alone own shares in DeBeers in the form of ADRs (American Depository Receipts). Although the price of their stock, like most South African companies, has been erratic, the dividends have more than made up for that. With the growing industrial uses of diamonds, there is every reason to expect continual profitability, even as gem production diminishes.

But an equally important part of the story is the strong underlying financial position of the company. DeBeers' ratio of debt to its total capitalization is only some 27 percent. In other words, it is not heavily dependent on creditors.

What's more, it has *cash* reserves, according to its 1978 consolidated balance sheet, of 1,294,898,000 rands (more than $1.56 billion)! And it has diamond stocks worth 255,630,000 rands ($309,312,300). Here is a very important key to DeBeers' control of the diamond market — its phenomenal ability to act as a spigot, turning on and off the diamond supply.

HOW THE CARTEL REGULATES THE MARKET

For the investor, the DeBeers cartel is of extensive significance. Through its benevolent hegemony, the organization has nearly eliminated the extreme volatility associated with most commodities markets. Its tremendous cash position enables it, when necessary, to go into the wholesale market and buy up cut stones and siphon them off the market, thus reducing supplies and bolstering prices. Normally, it would take this action after reducing the amount of rough goods it supplies to the market. On the other hand, its diamond inventories enable it, when and if necessary, to increase available supplies in order to counter too sharp a rise in prices.

Like the classical monopolist, DeBeers seeks to set prices at a level that is neither too low nor too high. If prices begin rising too fast this is a sign of potential instability. An illustration of this willingness and ability occurred in 1977. DeBeers found that many diamond merchants and cutters, particularly in inflation and trouble-ridden Israel, were hoarding the rough stones they had purchased at the CSO "sights" (sales) in London. High premiums (over and above the DeBeers prices for rough stones) developed, sometimes resulting in a doubling in price as the stone sat in vaults removed from an increasingly constricted marketplace.

In this instance, DeBeers solved the problem by, first of all, imposing a 40 percent, temporary surcharge on merchants at its March 28, 1978 "sight" offering. At the same time, some say not so coincidentally, financing of diamond inventories in Tel Aviv mysteriously began drying up. The net result was to flush out a greater number of stones from hoards and to dampen the speculative fever that threatened to destabalize DeBeers' carefully cultivated marketplace. More recently, DeBeers has followed this action by reducing the number of diamond dealers and cutters it invites to participate at its "sights." This underscored the cartel's case to prevent excessive price movements that could give way to price weakness later.

Until recently there were an estimated 250 so-called "sight holders." These are people — mostly representatives of diamond cutting factories, but also some brokers who sell to smaller cutters — who are privileged to come to the Central Selling Organization's Charterhouse Street headquarters in London approximately every five weeks and buy diamonds. A less important "sight" is also held in Kimberly, South Africa. As a disciplinary move, DeBeers terminated the buying privileges of some 25 direct buyers who were caught speculating in

1977 and 1978. Some say the figure is even higher. Once again, DeBeers strongly but deliberately served the best interests of the diamond market.

The London "sights," as these periodic congregations of the world's leading diamond factors are called, are unique and very intriguing phenomena.

Short of Fort Knox, it would be hard to find tighter security than one sees at the CSO's imposing London headquarters.

Within the walls of this fortress, guarded by electronic surveillance devices at every conceivable angle, the world's monthly production of gem quality, rough diamonds are sorted on long tables by workers facing the natural northern light coming in from windows. At any given time, upwards of a quarter of a billion dollars worth of uncut diamonds, ranging in size from one to two carats to over 100 carats, can be found within the walls of the Charterhouse Street edifice.

Every five weeks, the select sight holders make their pilgrimage there to replenish their larder of rough diamonds.

It is an exclusive club of men who are lucky enough to be invited to the "sights." Each participant is presented with a small box of rough stones, the size and quality varying, depending on the sight holder's weight in the industry and how well he is thought of by the unseen minions of the "Syndicate."

There are two categories of buyers from DeBeers: those who actually cut the rough stones, and those who are dealers in rough stones. The dealers perform an important, if lesser known, function: that of supplying rough diamonds to the smaller cutters who cannot afford to, or who are not allowed to, buy directly from DeBeers. Generally, these cutters, because they are buying from a dealer, pay a higher price for the rough diamonds.

Both dealers and cutters are free to survey the contents of the box. But they know that they should not quibble or complain too much. Nor should they refuse to accept the box designated

for them, lest they not be invited back again to Number 2 Charterhouse Street. The general needs and wishes of the "sight
holders" are conveyed to the CSO by way of brokers. But, by
and large, a DeBeers client takes what he is offered and pays
the price that is asked.

Why so much obsequiousness? Because, despite any rumors
to the contrary, DeBeers is THE SOURCE and probably the
cheapest source, for rough stones. And because each lucky participant knows that he is apt to make out very well with his particular box of stones. In fact, were it not for the paternal hand
of DeBeers, it is likely that many of the diamond cutters of
Antwerp, New York, and other cutting centers would long since
have gone out of business. Craftsmen they are. Businessmen,
oftentimes, they are not. DeBeers has made it almost impossible to lose money in the diamond industry, and so while they
may sometimes act like rebellious children, the members of the
industry are (deep down) loving and grateful.

In short, DeBeers has been a benevolent, paternalistic positive force in the diamond industry. It insures that those who
cooperate with the cartel make a steady and fair profit. The
company is profit-oriented and refuses to take a loss because of
inflation or currency devaluation. This assures inflation rate
and dollar devaluation.

RUSSIAN INTENTIONS AND DE BEERS

While the exact amounts of Russian diamonds are unknown,
it is generally assumed they have the second largest reserves of
diamonds in the world. The Russian supplies, therefore, must
be taken into account when assessing the long term outlook for
diamonds.

Starting in 1960, when the Soviets signed an agreement with
the company, DeBeers sold Russian diamonds at its London

sales offerings. But more recently, as the Soviet Union became self-conscious about its image in black Africa, it stopped dealing openly with the white South African-based company. Reportedly, the Russians now sell the bulk of their stones to DeBeers indirectly through Hambros Bank. In 1977, according to *National Geographic* magazine, Russian diamond sales through the DeBeers' "Syndicate" netted half a billion dollars.

No one knows the exact arrangement the Russians have with DeBeers at present, but there has been a lot of nervous speculation about it, based on fears that the Soviets might bolt the cartel and sell diamonds on their own directly to the cutters' market. Most knowledgeable insiders say that Russia operates under a contract with DeBeers, which is renegotiated and renewed annually. Reportedly, the Soviets have been pushing for a bigger share of the action from DeBeers and has been a major factor behind recent Syndicate price increases and surcharges.

There is evidence that the Soviets sell at least part of their stones (as yet a relatively small portion) outside cartel channels. The Soviet trading company Russalmaz, which is based in Moscow and has offices in Antwerp, Geneva, and Frankfurt, is known to have sold appreciable quantities of Siberian rough diamonds directly to cutters, both in Antwerp and New York.

But it is also believed that DeBeers, acting discreetly through middlemen, buys up some of the Russian rough, as well as other black market and non-cartel goods whenever it feels that excess supplies are coming onto the market outside its authorized channels. In this way, DeBeers even manages to control the remaining 15 or 20 percent of the diamond market it doesn't control directly!

Concern over Soviet intentions and Soviet actions is overwrought and a bit pointless. It simply would not make sense for the Soviet Union to do anything that would undermine the stability, indeed the upward bias, of diamond prices. For it benefits as much as any producer. It is extremely doubtful the Russians would like to supplant DeBeers as the central marketer of stones.

It is fair to say that they would like to get a high price for their diamonds. In fact, it is regularly reported that the Russians consistently press DeBeers to raise prices. Diamonds are a main hard currency earner for the Soviets, and their need for dollars, Deutsch Marks, Swiss francs, etc. is constantly increasing. In the absence of the control by DeBeers, the Soviets themselves would have to mount a comparable marketing effort that would be capable of duplicating the DeBeers' fine tuning of diamond prices. And the Russians realize they would probably fail. It is in their best long-term interest, therefore, for the Russians to continue to cooperate with DeBeers. And despite occasional growls from them, most experts expect that they will.

Another major concern about the Russians is that some day they and their puppet governments will take over Africa and its diamond riches. That would be a shame, but what if they do? There is every reason to believe that the result would be higher diamond prices than ever, if only because of the wave of fear this would create all over the world. But for now, it would be hard for even such a powerful nation as the Soviet Union (which has trouble financing its own grain imports) to imagine duplicating the role played by DeBeers.

CUTTING: TURNING PEBBLES INTO DIAMONDS

A very significant development of recent years has been the sudden emergence of DeBeers itself as a major factor in the cutting industry. Just as the Russians have done, DeBeers has apparently decided that it's not enough to be the major producer and the central marketer of rough stones. It wants also, apparently, to have a position, if not the dominant position, in the cutting of finished goods.

In other words, DeBeers is rapidly changing from a horizontal to a vertical organization. In five to ten years, I expect to see DeBeers being the largest manufacturer of finished diamonds. Already, the firm has indirect control of cut diamond prices by virtue of its influence over the supply of rough and its ability to regulate the amount of finished goods on the market through the use of its cash reserves and diamond inventories.

To the end of enlarging its influence on cut diamonds, DeBeers has established its own modern, sophisticated cutting factory in Portugal. It also reportedly has cutting facilities in Antwerp, Israel, and India. And it is now holding regular "sights" for finished diamonds in Lucerne, Switzerland. Hong Kong is rumored to be its next cut stone marketplace. Thus far, only about 25 buyers are participating in the Lucerne market, compared to the 225 at the rough "sights" in London. But, as DeBeers' role in the cutting business increases, these finished goods sights will also grow in importance. The net result should be even greater control of the market and diamond prices than before.

There are probably several hundred thousand cutters in the world, plying their trade in one of the five major cutting centers: Antwerp, New York, Tel Aviv, Bombay, and Johannesburg. Lesser centers include Rome, Paris, Frankfurt, and Rio de Janeiro. New York now cuts most of the larger stones of a carat and greater. Antwerp, which is still the leader, tends to specialize more and more in cutting the very big, expensive stones and, particularly, in cutting shapes other than the popular round, brilliant cut — designs such as the pear, marquise, and emerald cuts. Israel specializes in stones less than a carat in weight. And India, where an extimated 300,000 "cutters" labor, handles the tiniest "melee," stones as small as two points (2/100 of a carat).

Cutting "factories" are not quite what most people would imagine. The typical factory consists of a couple of small, dingy (but very tightly protected) rooms in an office building where perhaps a dozen cutters labor over cutting wheels. The world's largest diamond factory in Antwerp has about 150 cutters. But, despite the number of cutters cited above, a craftsman capable of cutting a fine stone is rare. The ability to bring out the full beauty of a rough diamond is a rare gift — a talent that is passed down from generation to generation.

It's a delicate art, both because of the nature of the material and because of the economics involved. Typically, half of the weight of the rough stone is lost in the cutting process. If a cutter can reduce that weight loss even by a few percent and increase the caratage sold, it can mean the difference between profit and loss. And it is a time-consuming process. An ordinary one-carat stone typically takes up to three weeks to cut. Larger, more expensive stones can take months.

Interestingly, in almost all diamond factories, the craftsmen are independent contractors, each carrying his own tools and even his own diamond "dust" for his polishing disc. Only the owner and managers of the factory are salaried employees. Every piece of work is done on a per stone basis, not per hour or per week or any other rate.

Upon getting their package of rough, a small supply that must suffice the cutting factory for two and a half months, the production manager or the cutters will carefully sort the stones and put them in individual envelopes, classified by weight and quality. Then he designs, from each piece of rough, the final shape of the finished stone.

With a practiced eye, he will determine how each stone should be cut and mark the stone with black India ink to guide the cutters in sawing and cutting the stone to yield maximum weight with optimum brilliance and minimum flaws. It's a tricky process, involving a large number of choices. Should a given rough stone be cut into one large or two little diamonds? Should a certain flaw or "inclusion" be avoided in order to produce a smaller or more perfect stone, or should a larger but less perfect stone be made? What should the exact proportions be relative to the size of the diamond? A shallower, more spread-out stone might yield less brilliance, but it would utilize more of the stone — and vice versa for a deeper, more brilliant, but smaller stone. And so forth.

The first step in this intricate and painstaking process is sawing or cleaving the rough stone to reduce it to pieces of the general size and shape that is desired. A stone can be broken, or cleaved, along the lines of its crystalline structure. But if the stone needs to be separated against that structure (against the grain in a sense) it must be sawed. The diamond is attached to a "do" and then cut along the marked lines with a rotating blade, whose cutting edge is coated with the diamond dust. This must be done carefully to avoid fracture, and sawing alone can take days.

Next, the stone is "girdled." At the stone's widest point, the stone is rounded to form as nearly a circular circumference as possible. This is done by rapidly rotating the stone and grinding its edges at the chosen diameter point against another diamond. Remember, only a diamond can cut another diamond.

After a round "girdle" has been achieved, the stone is "faceted" or "blocked." Both above and below the girdle, the stone is given its first four facets, yielding eight equal facets top and bottom — or a perfect octahedron. (Some rough stones come in that shape to begin with.) The stone may then be sawed again to knock off the top point of the octahedron and create a flat table. The facets are created by grinding the stone against a rotating table. The table is covered with a mixture of oil and diamond "dust," which tends to penetrate into the steel of the disc.

After the stone is given its first eight facets, the edges of those facets are ground to create a total of 16 facets. This is called "squaring." This process, which grows ever more minute as facets are subdivided, continues until there are a final 58 facets, including the "table" (top) and "culet" (the bottom of the diamond).

This is the so-called "round brilliant cut". It was given its modern-day ideal of mathematical perfection in 1919, by Marcel Tolkowsky, who wrote a book on how to cut diamonds for maximum scintillation. Today, the Tolkowsky cut has been somewhat updated by market forces, but much of his theory remains accepted as the model for diamonds. Regardless of your own aesthetics, it makes sense to have the type of stone that is in greatest demand and is therefore easier to liquidate when the time comes.

WORLDWIDE DIAMOND "BOURSES — THE STOCK MARKETS OF THE TRADE

Traditionally, however, the primary source of cut diamonds has been the diamond exchanges or "bourses". There are a total of 16 located in ten different countries, as listed below:

New York (two)	Johannesburg (one)	Tel Aviv (two)
Antwerp (four)	Milan (one)	London (two)
Paris (one)	Idar-Oberstein,	Amsterdam (one)
Vienna (one)	Germany (one)	

Many diamond deals are made at dealers' offices or even in the street in the major diamond districts, but the bourses play a pivotal role, especially in establishing prices. From New York to Tel Aviv, manufacturers and others come to these central locations to haggle with an assortment of buyers. Some rough is marketed here as well, by brokers with access to the DeBeers sights, to smaller cutters who are not able to participate in the sights.

But primarily it is a cut stone marketplace. The public is totally excluded from the Bourse. Membership in the exchanges is exclusive and is made up primarily of diamond brokers and cutters of long standing in the industry. The exchanges are governed both by a long tradition of trust and integrity and by the strict rules of the World Federation of Diamond Bourses. Wherever they are to be found, the bourses are fairly unimpressive looking places — little more than large, amply-lit rooms filled with long tables. Across these tables, buyer and seller can sit and bargain — and bargain, and bargain. The stones are examined with a "loupe," a ten times magnifying monocle that can be held in the eye socket. The bourse provides a scale for weighing.

When all the haggling is over, the deal is concluded with a handshake and the Yiddish words "Mazel und broche," which means "luck and blessing." Mutual trust and credit are the bywords. However, it is simply understood that by 10 a.m. the following day, the price of purchase must have been made — usually in cash — unless other terms of payment are agreed to. The diamonds are then sealed in small envelopes.

Occasionally disputes arise, and one of the most important functions of the bourses is to provide arbitration. Usually, the members in disagreement over a particular transaction will meet in the presence of two elected officials of the bourse, who will try to reconcile the differences. If they are unsuccessful, a three-man arbitration council is established to hear the case, and a decision is rendered. One appeal is allowed to yet another five-man arbitration body.

It is well known that anyone who commits deliberate fraud (or other unseemly acts) in a diamond transaction, or who refuses to abide by the arbitrators' decision, will be ostracized by the trade. Not only will he lose his membership in his particular bourse, but he will find himself unable to deal in the diamond industry anywhere in the world. This self-policing has been remarkably successful in keeping the closely-knit diamond industry clean.

CHANNELS OF DIAMOND DISTRIBUTION

The diamond industry, justifiably, seems mystifying to many people. From DeBeers to the jeweler on 47th Street in the heart of the New York diamond district, there are many different levels and gradations of function and expertise. There are very strict lines between cutting, brokering, wholesaling and retailing — four distinct disciplines.'' People who are cutters are not in the retail trade. And people who are retailers, in spite of what they say, are not in the cutting trade. (See **Figure 4**).

And, from level to level, there are tremendous changes in price, as the diamond winds its way ''from the mine to the mistress,'' as the old saying goes. As the diamond passes from the Central Selling Organization, to dealers, to cutters, through the Bourses, to cut stone brokers, to jewelry manufacturers, to wholesale jewelers, to retail jewelers, and finally to the customer, the price is apt to be increased anywhere from 275 to 300 percent, sometimes more.

The person who is interested in buying diamonds for investment obviously does not want to pay retail prices, such as he faces from his local jeweler. But where does he get into the picture? Unless he is making a very large purchase, and I'm talking about high six figures, he cannot hope to buy directly from a cutter. Unless you are a member of the family, cutters simply refuse to deal with customers. They are geared to deal in millions of dollars and usually do not wish to be bothered with transactions of $50,000 or even $100,000. Equally, they are

Figure 4.
Normal Distribution Channels
for Diamond Sales

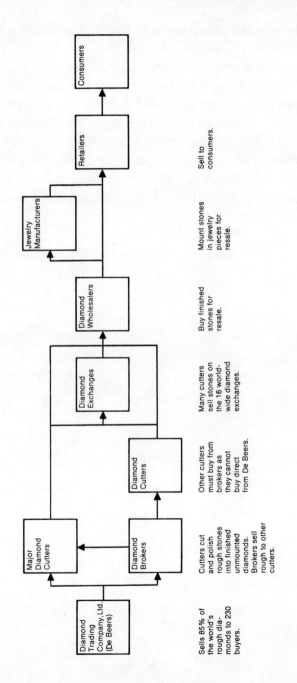

Source: Gemstone Trading Corporation

extremely worried about security and will not deal with an individual unknown to them.

That is why a relatively new factor has entered the diamond industry in recent years: the investment diamond dealer. The best of the investment diamond dealers are able to buy stones direct from a major cutter with a sight holding, or at least on one of the bourses, thus bypassing all of the price-escalating layers beneath the cutting stage. Shortly we'll look at some of the "dos" and "don'ts" of buying diamonds from this new breed. But first let's look at how diamonds are graded and priced.

5

"The Four C's" — Color, Clarity, Cut and Carat Weight

There are essentially four determinants of a diamond's value. In order of their importance they are: color, clarity, cut, and carat weight.

CARAT WEIGHT

All things being equal, a larger stone will naturally be more valuable. That is, if two stones have the same grades of color and clarity, and are cut with the same proportions, and one weighs two carats while the other weighs one carat, the two-carat stone will be worth more.

How much more? One might suspect that, in this instance, the two-carat stone's value would be double that of the one-carat stone. Not so. In practice, the value of a stone per carat goes up exponentially. Thus, a two-carat stone might be worth three times as much, instead of two times as much, as a one-carat diamond. The reason for this phenomenon is the greater rarity of larger stones. This is true of all weights.

A carat, which equals about 1/142 of an ounce, contains 100 points. Each point of weight is of tremendous importance in determining value. And just as there is a big difference in per carat value between a one-carat and a two-carat stone, so is there a big difference in value between a one-carat stone and less-than-a-carat stones. So, for instance, two 50-point (half-carat) stones would not equal the value of a single one-carat stone, even though the total weights would be the same. Significantly, according to industry standards, fractions of a point in weight are rounded down, not up. Thus, a 99.7-point diamond would be considered a 99-point diamond, not a one-carat diamond.

In the past, investors concentrated on one-carat diamonds; however, as the larger stones have become rarer and more expensive, diamonds of .50 carat and above have come into demand for investment purposes, both for smaller investors and for larger investors who desire to diversify their portfolios to include some smaller stones. There's a critical element involving weight that should be understood by investors — it's called the diamond "break points."

Diamonds are sold on a price per carat basis. For example, if a certain 1.08-carat diamond costs $20,000 per carat, the stone in question would cost $20,000 × 1.08, or $21,600. Not all cutters have the same price "break points," but the categories listed below can be considered generally followed by the trade. Stones of *exactly* the same quality, will sell at a different price per carat as you move into a different range. Within any given range, to get a stone's price, simply multiply the per carat price by the carat weight.

Price Break Points

(All stones of the same color, clarity, cut and shape in
each category should be roughly the same *price per
carat.)*

0.48 – 0.64
0.65 – 0.79
0.80 – 0.88
0.89 – 0.94
----*
1.00 – 1.39
1.39 – 1.48
1.49 – 1.69
1.70 – 1.99
2.00 – 2.49
2.50 – 2.99
3.00 – 3.99
etc.

*Prices and breakpoints of stones between .95 – .99 vary
substantially between cutters and at the bourses. Sup-
ply/demand is the most important determining factor. A
stone of .99, for example, could easily sell for 25% more
than a stone of the exact same quality weighing .95. And a
.99 diamond will sell for 10-20 percent less than a stone of
the same quality weighing exactly 1.00 ct.

But carat weight is still only of relative importance. The internal and external characteristics of the diamond — color (the
degree of whiteness or colorlessness), clarity (the degree of
flawlessness), and cut (the degree to which the diamond con-
forms to accepted proportion standards) make all the difference. Two similar-looking one-carat diamonds of exactly

the same weight can vary by as much as $40,000 per carat by virtue of slightly differing quality features.

For any given size, the other three factors break down this way. Color is by far the most important determinant, making up about 50 percent of the average stone's value. Clarity and cut are about equally important, making up 25 percent each of the remaining value.

This 50–25–25 breakdown might seem to leave no room for the weight factor. In fact weight is of great importance but only in comparing stones in the context of their other qualities. The best way to illustrate this is by example.

Let's say you're trying to choose between a one-carat stone and a two-carat stone and they both have the same price tag. Obviously in this case the higher color, clarity, and cut grades of the smaller stone outweigh the size of the bigger one.

On the other hand, one might expect a two-carat "flawless", white diamond to be double the value of a one-carat diamond of comparable quality. But in fact the value would be more than double. This is because larger stones of any grade are rarer.

Finally, take two stones of the *same weight,* but of *different grades.* Weight in this example has little importance.

With the rare exceptions of "fancy" diamonds (the pinks, blues, canary yellows, and so forth), when we speak of color in diamonds we are really speaking ideally of a lack of color. In recent years, as laboratory techniques and equipment improved, the grading of color has been increasingly refined.

COLOR

Traditionally, color was graded in broad categories. For instance the old Scandinavian system's top grade was "River," equivalent to the old British "blue white" category. Today, under color grading standards developed first by the Gemological Institute of America (G.I.A.), that category is broken down into three smaller grades: "D", "E" and "F".

Figure 5 shows a comparison between the various color grading systems most prominently in use around the world. The most important for American investors are those of the G.I.A. and the E.G.L. (the European Gemological Laboratory). Interestingly, the E.G.L. has taken to printing on its grading certificates not only its own numbered color grade, but also, in parentheses, the equivalent G.I.A. letter grade. Because these systems are more detailed and exact, an investor would be well-advised to adhere to and seek them out, rather than risk the much vaguer and often abused vertical descriptions. If someone offers you a "blue white" stone for example, run, don't walk, away from the deal.

An exception is the word scale used by the highly respected Hoge Raad Voor Diamant (HRD), the Antwerp-based laboratory of the Belgian High Diamond Council. This scale was approved in May 1978 by the Congress of World Federation of Diamond Bourses and the International Diamond Manufacturers Association. Luckily, as far as combating confusion is concerned, the HRD's word descriptions of color — "exceptional white + ," "exceptional white," "rare white," and so forth — correspond closely to the letter and number grades of the G.I.A. and E.G.L., as can be seen in the chart. Not until you get to color grades below "H" (G.I.A.) or "2" (E.G.L.), is there variation. "I" and "J" ("3" and "4") are combined in a category called "slightly tinted white" by HRD. The next two color grades are also united, as you can see. But this presents little problem for the investor, who is mainly concerned with grades "H" and above anyway.

Color grades range from colorless down to obvious tints of yellow, which come from nitrogen and other impurities, but between those two extremes, the gradations are almost im-

Figure 5.
Comparison of Different Color Grading Systems

	G.I.A.	E.G.L.	H.R.D.	A.G.S.*	SCAN D.N.* (.50 carats & above)
COLOR-LESS	D	0+	EXCEPTIONAL WHITE +	0	RIVER
COLOR-LESS	E	0	EXCEPTIONAL WHITE	0	RIVER
COLOR-LESS	F	1+	RARE WHITE +	1	
NEARLY COLOR-LESS	G	1	RARE WHITE		TOP WESSELTON
NEARLY COLOR-LESS	H	2	WHITE	2	WESSELTON
NEARLY COLOR-LESS	I	3	SLIGHTLY TINTED WHITE	3	TOP CRYSTAL
NEARLY COLOR-LESS	J	4	SLIGHTLY TINTED WHITE	4	CRYSTAL
SLIGHTLY TINTED	K	5	TINTED WHITE	5	TOP CAPE
SLIGHTLY TINTED	L	6	TINTED WHITE	6	TOP CAPE
SLIGHTLY TINTED	M	7			CAPE
SLIGHTLY TINTED	N	8		7	CAPE
VERY LIGHT YELLOW	O	9			
VERY LIGHT YELLOW	P	10		8	LIGHT YELLOW
VERY LIGHT YELLOW	Q	11	TINTED COLOR	8	LIGHT YELLOW
LIGHT YELLOW	R	12			
LIGHT YELLOW	S	13			
LIGHT YELLOW	T	14		9–10	YELLOW
YELLOW	U	15			YELLOW
YELLOW	V	16			

FINEST GEM QUALITY (D–J)

GENERAL COMMERCIAL QUALITY (K–V)

*AMERICAN GEM SOCIETY
*SCANDINAVIAN DIAMOND NOMENCLATURE

WHILE THE G.I.A. SCALE REPRESENTS THE MOST UNIVERSALLY USED SYSTEM, OTHER INTERNATIONALLY ACCEPTED SCALES EXIST. THE ABOVE CHART COMPARES THESE.

perceptible. To the untrained eye of the layman a stone may appear colorless all the way down to the grade of "J", which is considered to be at the bottom of the range of grades called "near colorless ("G" through "J" on the G.I.A. scale, "1" through "4" on the E.G.L. scale). That grade may be fine, as far as appearance is concerned, for engagement rings or other jewelry purposes, but an investor must be more discerning.

Color grades considered best for investment are "D" through "H" on the G.I.A. scale, which corresponds to "0+ through "2" on the E.G.L. scale. You should always insist on a certificate from a recognized and reputable gemological laboratory that attests to one of those color grades. However, if you wish to personally examine the diamonds you are considering buying, you should be aware of the conditions that are considered by the trade as ideal for grading color.

The traditional method of judging true color was by viewing a stone under natural, north sunlight; however, sunlight isn't always dependable. Most laboratories nowadays use a controlled, fluorescent lighting environment. This eliminates the effect of ultra-violet fluorescence. Some fluorescence in a stone is not bad, and it doesn't necessarily detract from a stone's value, so long as it is pervasive in a stone and is not concentrated in a single area. Fluorescence may even enhance a diamond's "fire" or brilliance, but it shouldn't interfere with your judgment or the gemologist's judgment of the stone's true color.

A stone is usually color graded by viewing the stone unmounted, from the top, that is by looking straight down on its table (the broad flat facet on the top of the round, brilliant cut diamond). The background should be white. And, above all, regardless of the lighting employed, the diamond should be compared side-by-side against a set of master stones. This is a carefully selected array of stones from each color grade, which the grader can use to compare and contrast with the diamond being examined. Often, gemologists use a photospectroscope to analyze color more scientifically by measuring exactly a stone's nitrogen content.

The layman should never deceive himself about being able to judge for himself the true color of a stone. Anyone who thinks he can is just kidding himself. And the stakes are very high. The dollar difference between a "D" and an "H" one-carat flawless stone is around $50,000. Tricky lighting techniques can easily fool an unpracticed eye. The bottom line is still a dependence on the reputation of the person who is selling you the diamond and of the grading certificate that should accompany it.

CLARITY

Clarity is an equally subtle, though slightly less significant, factor in a diamond's value. Clarity refers to the number and size of flaws or "inclusions" in a diamond. There are a number of different types of "inclusions." Some diamonds may actually have a tiny crystal within them. Sometimes they look like bubbles. Others may show a crack along the stone's crystal structure. Others may show "feathers" within, which are tiny fractures. Some diamonds have spots of black or brown within them, called "carbon spots." Or there may be "clouds", which are close groupings of small crystals or bubbles. A concentrated area of fluorescence is also considered a flaw or inclusion. In fact, anything that deters the passage of light through a stone is considered a flaw.

The internationally accepted measurement for clarity must be done under 10-power magnification. If no flaws can be seen at that degree of magnification, the diamond is deemed to be flawless, the highest possible clarity grade a diamond can obtain. It is important that the stone not be mounted when inspected, as the setting can hide imperfections.

But before arriving at that determination, a laboratory gemologist will usually turn his microscope up to 40-power or even higher to view the diamond's flaws. After locating any inclusions that may be there, he then reduces the magnification back down to ten. If, at that power, the flaws can no longer be seen, then the stone is adjudged to be "flawless." If some flaws can still be seen at that power, then the grading is reduced. Therefore, the international yardstick for judging clarity is 10-power magnification. No more, no less.

Incidentally, it takes an experienced gemologist to do this. A trick of the brain and the optic nerve tends to afflict the average person, so that anything seen at 40-power or higher tends to imprint inself in the mind, so that it can still be seen even when the microscope is returned to the lower degree of magnification. By the same token, what you can see with your naked eye is meaningless. A stone may look flawless and yet contain enough flaws to reduce its value by tens of thousands of dollars.

Figure 6 depicts the clarity grading system used by the diamond trade both here and in Europe. The G.I.A., E.G.L., and HRD use the same nomenclature for grading clarity, although there may be differences in *how* they grade. The HRD, for instance, tends to rely more heavily on quantitative measurements, specifying how many microns a flaw can be in size in order to qualify a diamond for a certain clarity category.

But generally speaking, the clarity grades are defined as follows:

"Flawless" — This, of course, is the ultimate clarity grade. The description means that, under 10-power magnification (either with a microscope or jeweler's loupe), neither internal nor external flaws can be seen. That is, there are neither surface scratches or blemishes, nor inclusions within the body of the diamond. The definition does permit an extra facet on the pavilion (the bottom of the stone) so long as it cannot be seen

Figure 6.
G.I.A. Clarity-Grading Scale

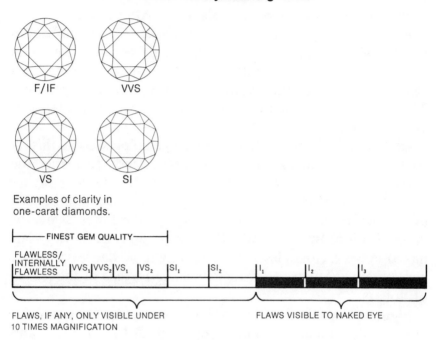

Examples of clarity in
one-carat diamonds.

Source: Gemstone Trading Corporation

when the stone is viewed from the top, looking straight down on the table. Also permitted is a minor "natural," which is a remaining bit of the original rough stone's surface, on the edge of the girdle. (That's the circumference around the base of the crown which divides the top of the diamond from the bottom.) Finally, growth or "twin" lines along the crystal's structure are allowed, so long as they do not reach the outer surface and so long as they do not distort the color or passage of light.

It should be noted that the G.I.A. and E.G.L. almost never issue a "Flawless" certificate. Inevitably, there will be a microscopic finishing blemish on the exterior of the diamond during the cutting process. The blemish disqualifies the diamond for the "Flawless" designation. For all intents and purposes, "Internally Flawless" is the top clarity grade. Furthermore, there is almost no price difference between a "Flawless" and "Internally Flawless" diamond.

Just as the name signifies, an "Internally Flawless" stone must meet the same *internal* criteria as the first category, "Flawless," but the surface of the cut stone is more flawed. It may have too many extra facets, finish blemishes, cutting marks, too many or too obvious "naturals", and so forth.

"VVS$_1$" and "VVS$_2$" — These are two gradations of the "very, very small inclusions" category, the first grade below "flawless." Stones in this category have tiny flaws that even an expert using 10-power magnification has great difficulty detecting. "VVS" is subdivided into "VVS$_1$" and "VVS$_2$", the former being the higher grade, the latter the lower. A "VVS$_1$" has even more minute and hard-to-find inclusions than does a "VVS$_2$." The location of the internal flaws is also an important determinat of which "VVS" grade a stone is given. If the inclusions are on the periphery of the stone, away from the central area under the table, then it is usually called a "VVS$_1$," assuming the flaws are small enough. If the flaws are still minute, but are located more centrally, and therefore more in the way of light refraction, then the stone is apt to be given the slightly lower grade of "VVS$_2$." Further, surface scratches and blemishes must be very minor.

"VS$_1$" and "VS$_2$" — These are stones with "very small inclusions," defined as flaws that are still difficult for the gemologist to locate under 10-power magnification, but less so than for the previous grade. That is, the inclusions are a bit larger than those in "VVS" stones. Finish imperfections may also be a bit more significant but still relatively minor.

"S$_1$ and "S$_2$" — These are stones with "small inclusions." But by this stage, the flaws are easy ("S$_1$") or very easy ("S$_2$") to detect under the microscope. They still cannot be seen with the naked eye, but they are big enough to detract substantially from the passage of light, and hence the brilliance of the diamond. Sometimes this grade is also called "slightly imperfect." In fact, some people substitute "imperfect" for "inclusion" throughout the clarity scale. But imperfection, as opposed to "inclusion," is a tricky term. Even a "flawless" diamond, under the widely accepted definition given above, is not "perfect" (or faultless) in the true sense.

"I_1," "I_2, and "I_3 — These are stones with readily apparent inclusions — often generally termed "Piqué." These are stones whose inclusions are visible in one way or another, to the naked eye.

It is generally recommended that investors should purchase only diamonds in the "Flawless" through "VS_1" grade range.

CUT

The last of our "Four C's" is "cut," which means not so much the general design of the diamond but the way a stone is proportioned for optimum use of light and the way the stone is finished or polished. Cut also refers to the shape of the diamond. The round brilliant cut is the most desirable design for investment purposes. It is the classic standard and should remain so well into the future. **Figure 7** diagrams the various parts of the round brilliant cut. The way each of these parts is proportioned in relationship to each other and in relationship to the total diamond is extremely important in determining the diamond's appearance.

Cutting a diamond for maximum brilliance (maximum light refraction and reflection) is not as simple and straightforward as it may seem. Although there are carefully designed mathematical formulas for cutting the ideal diamond to minimize light "leakage," there are other economic considerations.

To produce the ideal shape and proportions may require

Figure 7.
Standard Measurement Nomenclature for Gem-Quality Diamonds

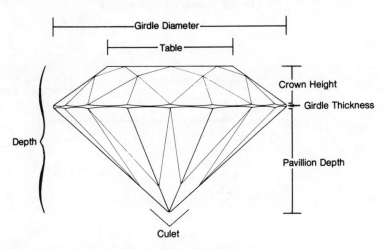

unacceptable sacrifices of weight. And if a given piece of rough contains strategically placed flaws, the cutter has an even more difficult choice to make. Most stones are a compromise between the three considerations of maximizing weight, optimizing proportions, and minimizing inclusions. Then too, there are variations of preferences between the United States and Europe. As a result, there is almost no such thing as *the* ideal, perfectly shaped stone. The best one can do is strive to buy a stone that is as close to the ideal as possible. There is a range of proportions that are considered acceptable, and these "ranges" are called "tolerances."

Figure 8 shows the importance of shape and proportion, as the lines indicate how light will be treated by various shapes. On both extremes — deep and shallow — a diamond tends to "leak" light out the side and bottom. The result, of course, is that little light is reflected back out through the top of the diamond, and the diamond appears flat and dull — without the fire, brilliance, and sparkle that are critical to its appearance.

Figure 8.
Passage of Light Through
Three Types of Diamonds

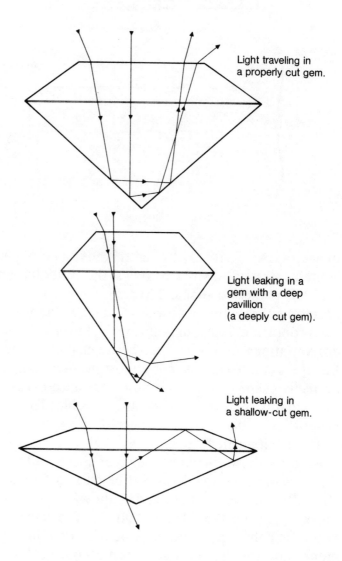

Light traveling in
a properly cut gem.

Light leaking in a
gem with a deep
pavillion
(a deeply cut gem).

Light leaking in
a shallow-cut gem.

It is impossible that every diamond be cut to perfect proportions, but there are generally accepted ranges, or "tolerances," that fall within international standards. A diamond whose critical proportions are substantially outside these tolerances should be avoided for investment purposes. It's not that they won't appreciate in value — they will. It's just that the investor must try to stay within as narrow a range as possible when dealing with an item so esoteric as diamonds. The strategy is to buy quality — get the best.

The tolerances listed in **Figure 9** are acceptable just about anywhere in the world. I recommend staying with that which is known and easily salable.

Figure 10 shows the ideally cut diamond with each of the dimensions and angles clearly shown. As can be seen in the diagram, all of the important measurements relate to the diameter of the stone (at its widest point — the girdle). The critical angles and proportions are defined and quantified, by investment standards, as follows:

Girdle thickness — The girdle is the circumference of the diamond, the edge going all around the diamond. The thickness of the girdle should not be "very thick" or "extremely thick". "Thin" to "slightly thick" is acceptable. Closer to "medium" is preferable. And the girdle should be relatively even. That is, there should not be more than a two-to-four degree difference in the thickness of the girdle edge from its thinnest to its thickest point.

Table — The large facet at the top of the stone, which is the flat surface that presents itself to the eye of the beholder, is the table. It is measured in terms of what percentage the table, at its widest point, is of the diameter. The girdle diameter is, by definition, 100 percent. The table width is then some smaller percentage of that. Marcel Tolkowsky, the father of the round brilliant cut, set the ideal table diameter at 53 percent of the girdle diameter in 1919. In 1970, the Scandinavian proposal for

Figure 9.
Internationally Accepted Tolerances For
Proportions of Gem-Quality Diamonds

Acceptable Tolerances		Ideal
Depth	57–63%	60%
Table	57–66%	60–63%
Culet	None, Small, Medium	Small
Polish	Good, Fair to Good	Good
Symmetry	Good, Fair to Good	Good
Girdle	Very Thin, Thin, Medium, Thick, Slightly Thick, Faceted, or 2–4%	Thin or Medium
Graining	Slight, Surface, Significant	Nil (but only in Flawless)
Ultraviolet Fluorescent	Varies from country to country. In U.S. — most grades are acceptable. In some cases color is improved by high degree of fluorescence. Slight to medium acceptable.	None or Slight
Crown Height	11–16% } On E.G.L. certificates only	13%
Pavilion Depth	40–46% }	43%
Comments:	Hairline feathers in girdle	None
	Minor details of polish not shown	None
	(Many other items which do not affect value are often listed on certificate under the "comment" section)	

Crown angles less than 30% or greater than 35% <u>unacceptable</u> (on G.I.A. certificates only)	Between 30% and 35%

Europe set the ideal table proportion at 57.5 percent. However, most people prefer an even wider table. Generally, in a one-carat diamond, the market places the highest premium on table within a range of 57 to 66 percent. In a half or three-quarter-carat diamond, the range is somewhat narrower — 57 to 65 percent.

Depth — Depth refers to the length (or height) of the diamond from table to culet (top to bottom) as a percentage of the diameter of the diamond at the girdle. Tolkowsky's ideal formula called for a 59.3 percent depth. The Scandinavian ("Scan. D.N.") ideal is 57.7 percent. The generally acceptable range for investors is 57 to 63 percent. Somewhere in between, preferably 60 percent, is the market's preferred depth proportion at the moment.

Figure 10.
Acceptable Range of Tolerances for Well-Cut
Gem-Quality, Round Brilliant Diamonds

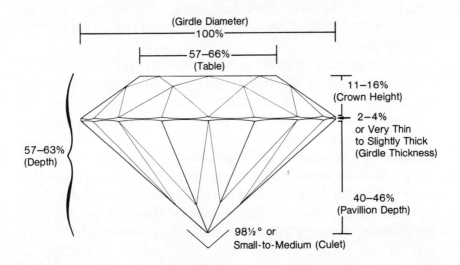

Crown Height or Crown Angles — The crown, which is the faceted area between the girdle and the table, can be measured in one of two ways. Usually a certificate will indicate the crown height as a percentage of the girdle's diameter — if it mentions it at all. As this is written, only the E.G.L. uses crown measurements. Tolkowsky's ideal was that the crown height be 16.2 percent of the depth. The Scan. D.N. standard is 14.6 percent. An acceptable range is thought to be anywhere from 11 to 16 percent. Another way of measuring the crown is to measure the angle between the incline of the top — the slant of the crown — and the girdle. The G.I.A. certificate currently measures crown angles. This angle should not be less than 30 degrees or more than 35 degrees. If the diamond has acceptable crown angles, then no mention is made on the G.I.A. certificate. Of course, the crown, like the pavilion (the bottom) is subsumed by the total depth. It is still important, but considerably less so than either table or depth.

Culet — The culet is the point at the bottom of the diamond. It should be "small" to "medium". "Large" is unacceptable. And it should be on center relative to the top of the diamond, otherwise the angles of the pavilion will be off and light leakage will result.

Of course, none of these proportions can really be looked at in isolation. All of the proportions are interdependent within the overall design of the stone. The wider the table, the shallower the depth and vice versa. A higher depth yields a fuller crown, and so on.

Another proportion that is included on some certificates is the **pavilion depth.** This corresponds to the crown height, except that it is on the bottom of the stone, below the girdle. All it is, is the distance between the girdle and the culet as a percentage of the diameter. Acceptable ranges of pavilions are 40 to 46 percent.

There are two other characteristics of cut that you should be aware of and pay attention to: "polish" and "symmetry" (sometimes called proportion). Polish means the final, external finish of the diamond. It can be very important to a stone's refracting index. After the diamond is cut, it is polished to smooth out any nicks. The finish is given an overall, verbal grade. The top of the line is "good," diminishing to "fair-to-good," "fair," and "poor." "Good" is most desirable of course, but "fair-to-good" is acceptable. Symmetry is the degree to which the various angles and facets line up — the degree to which, in other words, the diamond is well-centered and well-proportioned in an overall sense. The word grading on symmetry is the same as polish — good, fair-to-good, fair, poor. Here again, good and fair-to-good are acceptable.

Having provided all these criteria, let me add a few comments. First of all, once again, it will be difficult for the novice to make his own judgment on the cut of a stone based simply on an eyeball inspection. Laboratory gemologists grade the proportions of a diamond with the help of an instrument known as a proportionscope, which enables him to enlarge the image of the stone under examination, make precise geometric calculations and, compare the results with the ideal measurements.

The importance of cut is not to be slighted. If a diamond deviates substantially from the ideal, significant loss of value results. But, at the same time, many investors-turned-overnight-experts make the mistake of stubbornly insisting on a certain ideal table or depth or crown proportion that may, especially in today's tight market, prove impossible to get at any price.

Finally, to reiterate, each of the "Four C's" presents an obstacle of knowledge to the novice. The average layman cannot really expect to make any valid quality judgments for himself. At the same time, on the other hand, he cannot be expected to feel comfortable in blindly and meekly placing himself in the hands of a seller whom he knows little about. So any knowledge the investor has will add to his ability to invest wisely and confidently.

That is where a fifth "C" comes in: Certification. It is the subject of our next chapter.

6

Certification — "The Fifth C"

In the past century, there have been three great developments in the diamond industry.

One was the discovery and exploitation of the vast African diamond deposits. Second came the introduction by DeBeers of a centrally controlled marketing mechanism for all world production. Finally, and perhaps most importantly for modern day investors, came the introduction and gradual acceptance of standards for grading, certifying, and identifying diamonds.

It all started in 1931, when the Gemological Institute of America was established. The going wasn't easy for the fledgling diamond grading laboratory at first, but gradually the G.I.A.'s grading standards gained wide acceptance. Operating independently of any other side of the industry and using increasingly scientific methods to refine the grading standards we talked about in Chapter 5, the G.I.A. gained a reputation for objectivity and consistency. And its certificates came to be increasingly demanded in diamond transactions along with the bill of sale.

In truth, it wasn't until this decade that G.I.A. certificates achieved full recognition and usage, but the explosion of interest in diamonds as an investment by the public necessitated certification as a means of assuring the investor some measure of protection. Soon, The G.I.A. found that it could not meet the demand for its certificates, even with three laboratories nationwide.

Competitors sprang up. In 1975, the European Gemological Laboratory (E.G.L.) was established in Antwerp. It now has labs in Antwerp, New York, and Los Angeles and grades some 100 stones per day in New York alone. The E.G.L., which based its grading standards on those of the G.I.A. and continues to follow them, has been responsible for some of the latest refinements in diamond grading. It has begun to provide more information about cut proportions and other characteristics on its certificates. It also seals both the stone and a microfilm copy of the certificate within a vinyl package to insure the authenticity of the graded stone. This prevents "switching" — sometimes a problem with diamonds.

In Europe, the Hoge Raad Voor Diamant (HRD) has evolved its own standards resembling those of the G.I.A. and E.G.L. The HRD lab was established by the Belgian Diamond Council, a semi-official body which is the most important diamond trade association in Belgium. The lab, therefore, has tremendous importance, and its certificates are as highly prized in Europe as the G.I.A. and E.G.L. Today, these three laboratories provide a worldwide pedigree for diamonds they grade. Yet another lab, The International Gemological Institute (IGI), opened a New York office in 1980. The IGI was established in 1975, and enjoys a good reputation in Europe. (For complete addresses of all the laboratories, see the appendix.)

A sort of de facto division of labor has emerged among the laboratories. In the carat sizes, that is, stones of one carat and greater, the market almost exclusively belongs to the G.I.A., except in Europe where the HRD is equally prominent, with its impeccable credentials. For stones weighing less than a carat, the market has come to be dominated by the E.G.L., largely because the G.I.A. has almost stopped grading those size stones entirely.

The E.G.L. also grades stones above one carat, but even though its standards are as good as the G.I.A.'s, there has been a tendency for carat-size stones not graded by the G.I.A. to sell at a discount of as much as ten percent. This discount on E.G.L.-certified one-carat stones, which is a natural consequence of the G.I.A.'s decades-old tradition of dominance, seems to be disappearing, however.

Anyone can send a diamond to one of these labs for grading and certification. The G.I.A. and the other labs have a sliding scale of charges for their services. For instance, the G.I.A. currently charges $55 to certify a one-carat stone and $80 for a two-carat stone. The E.G.L. charges $30 per carat for certification, plus $10 for the special E.G.L. seal. Stones under a carat are considered to be one carat for purposes of certification fees. Verification, which simply means verifying that a stone and its certificate match, costs 75 percent of the normal fee at the G.I.A.

It is important to distinguish between grading and appraisal. None of the labs mentioned here appraise stones. That is, they do not put a dollar value on the stones that they grade. They merely attest to the quality of the stone — the specifics of the "Four C's" discussed in the last chapter. It is then up to the owner of the diamond to place a value on the diamond. How this is done — for the purpose of selling — will be discussed shortly.

Although the laboratories do not set prices on the diamonds they grade, they have made diamond pricing and price comparisons much more objective, uniform, and reliable. Some, though not all, of the guesswork has been taken out of the buying and selling of diamonds. In fact, because of this, there was resistance from segments of the diamond industry, for a time, to the introduction of sophisticated grading standards and certification, for it meant that no longer could the diamond merchant, whatever his intentions, simply declare a diamond to be of such and such a quality (using vague word descriptions) and set a price accordingly. Certification has made it possible, to a much greater extent than ever before, for the layman to securely buy and sell diamonds because there is more uniformity in grading and pricing.

Certification is now accepted and used throughout the trade. Many a New York cutter and broker has told me that the availability of certificates has revolutionized the business, making diamond purchases more dependable for the average person. Probably the most important factor in winning the acceptance for certification has been the investment diamond dealers. They, more than anyone else, have promoted and propagated certification.

But, while investment diamond dealers have consulted laboratory certificates, many misuses of certificates by some of the less reputable firms that are in the business have occurred. The most common offense is the bogus certificate put out by the firm itself. More on that later, but suffice it to say, for now, that it is very important to get a certificate with your stone from one of the laboratories mentioned above. Do not buy a stone "graded according to G.I.A. standards" or by "G.I.A.-trained gemologists." The diamond should have a certificate from the lab itself. *Accept no substitutes.*

How do you read a certificate? Look at the facsimiles of a G.I.A. certificate and an E.G.L. certificate in **Figures 11** and **12**. Since the E.G.L. certificate has more information, let's look at it in some detail. (First, note that the certificate, just a specimen, is dated and coded.)

A. Weight — This is the weight in carats of the diamond. Since this diamond is less than a carat (0.87 carat), it could be expressed as 87 points.

B. Shape and Cut — The diamond referred to on the certificate is the common, popular round, brilliant cut, so all of the proportions referred to on the certificate will apply to that type of design, as discussed in Chapter 5.

C. Measurements — There are two sets of figures, expressed

Figure 11.
E.G.L. Certificate Facsimile

DIAMOND CERTIFICATE

issued by the

EUROPEAN GEMOLOGICAL LABORATORY™
pvba

Antwerp   **New York**   **Los Angeles**

Independent educational organisation.
Institute for certification of diamonds and precious stones.

Laboratory report	This examination has been scientifically carried out by a graduate gemmologist and may be repeated at any time.
Certificate N° *SAMPLE*	

Description:	*NATURAL DIAMOND*	*SAMPLE*
WEIGHT:	*0. 87 ct.*	
Shape and cut:	*ROUND BRILLIANT CUT*	
Measurements:	*Approx. Max 6. 06 Min 5. 99 x 3. 82 mm.*	
Proportions:	*GOOD*	
Depth %:	*63. 8%*	
Table diameter %:	*58%*	
Crown height:	*16%*	
Pavilion depth:	*44%*	
Girdle thickness:	*MEDIUM POLISHED*	
Finish grade:	*GOOD*	
PURITY*: (Clarity grade)	*VVS2*	
COLOR GRADE:	*1+(F)*	

Photoluminescence:	*NONE*
Comments:	

Laboratory director

Date: *May 31, 1980*

* (10 x Magnification)

Colour grade based on master comparison stones.
The laboratory does not and may not appraise
the stones which are submitted for its inspection.

ORIGINAL This report is rendered at the request of the customer submitting the above registered stone and is for his exclusive use. The report or seal expresses an opinion at the time of inspection of the stone, not a guarantee, valuation or appraisal. No representation or warranties as to the accuracy are made. E.G.L. is expressly held harmless by customer including, but without limitation for any claims or actions that may arise out of negligence in connection with preparation of this laboratory report or seal, or actions based upon the customer's use of the certificate or seal.

European Gemological Laboratory Inc

N° 91655

Figure 12.
G.I.A. Certificate Facsimile

Gemological Institute of America
GEM TRADE LABORATORY
Scientific Identification of Gemstones and Pearls

Diamond Report
No. NY123106
4/8/77

In the opinion of the Laboratory, the following are the characteristics of the stone, or stones, described on the attached report as based on measurements and also on observations made through the Gemolite (10X binocular darkfield magnification) and in the DiamondLite, utilizing master comparison stones. Mounted stones graded only to the extent that mounting permits examination.

(Red symbols denote internal characteristics, green, external. Symbols indicate nature and position of characteristics, not necessarily their size. Where applicable, setting prongs are shown by black symbols.)

SHAPE AND CUT ___ round brilliant
Measurements ___ approx. 6.73 - 6.82 X 4.09 mm
Weight ___ 1.15 carats

Key to symbols

-pinpoint inclusion
-feather

PROPORTIONS
Depth Percentage ___ 60.3%
Table Diameter Percentage ___ 65%
Girdle Thickness ___ slightly thin to medium, faceted
Culet Size ___ small

FINISH
Polish ___ good
Symmetry ___ good

CLARITY GRADE ___ VVS$_1$

COLOR GRADE ___ F
Ultraviolet fluorescence ___ none

COMMENTS:

Minor hairline feathers in girdle and details of polish not shown.

SPECIMEN

GEM TRADE LABORATORY
Gemological Institute of America

By ___

GIA CLARITY-GRADING SCALE

Flawless	VVS$_1$	VVS$_2$	VS$_1$	VS$_2$	SI$_1$	SI$_2$	I$_1$	I$_2$	I$_3$

Imperfect

GIA COLOR-GRADING SCALE

D	E	F	G	H	I	J	K	L	M	N	O	P	Q	R	S	T	U	V	W	X	Y	Z

Colorless	Near Colorless	Faint Yellow	Very Light Yellow	Light Yellow	Fancy Yellow

(Copyright 1975, GIA)

thusly: "max. 6.06 min. 5.99 x 3.82 mm." The first set of numbers refers to the diameter of the stone, expressed in millimeters. 6.06 mm. is the widest point of the stone (measured around the girdle), and 5.99 mm. is the narrowest point. In other words, the stone is not perfectly round; almost no stone is perfectly round, and nearly all stones will show two figures for the diameter. 3.82 mm. is the height of the diamond from table to culet.

D. Proportions — This refers to the symmetry of the stone, the general shape and configuration of facets and angles.

E. Depth % — 63.8 is the ratio of the height or length of the diamond to the diameter at the girdle.

F. Table Diameter % — This figure (58%) is the width of the table (the large, flat, eight-sided facet on top of the diamond) at its widest point relative to the total diameter of the diamond at the girdle.

G. Crown Height — This 16 percent expresses the ratio of the distance between the table and the girdle (the crown) to the distance between the table and the culet.

H. Pavilion Depth — This is the other part that, together with crown height, makes up the total depth percentage, with the small addition of girdle thickness (I). Pavilion is the area below the girdle, which comes to a point at the culet. The perpendicular distance from the girdle to the culet taken as a percentage of the total length of the diamond, is the pavilion depth.

I. Girdle Thickness — The girdle of the stone this certificate refers to has "medium" thickness and has been polished. Some cutters do not bother to polish the girdle. The girdle separates the crown (top of the stone) from the pavilion (bottom of the stone), and its thickness, which should be fairly even all around its circumference, is a small factor in the total depth percentage of the diamond.

J. Finish Grade — Also known as "polish," this grade refers to the condition of the diamond's surface area. This stone has been given the top grade of "good."

K. Purity (Clarity Grade) — The stone was given a grade of "VVS$_2$." This stands for "very, very slight inclusions," and because the inclusions or flaws were relatively easy to detect and relatively centered in the stone, it rated the grade of VVS$_2$ within the VVS category, instead of VVS$_1$. (See **Figure 6).** The inclusions referred to are marked on the diagram at the center right of the certificate. The left diagram is a top view of the stone. The right diagram is a bottom view. The inclusions, which have been somewhat exaggerated in size here in order to be visible, are placed by the gemologist at the exact spots on the diagram where they appear in the actual stone.

L. Color Grade — The E.G.L. has its own numbered, color-grading system. (See **Figure 5).** This stone has a 1+ grade, which corresponds to the G.I.A.'s "F." And that is given in parentheses. This particular grade means that the diamond is in the third best grade of the "colorless" category.

M. Photoluminescence — Often a diamond will have traces of luminescence that can be detected in ultra violet light. Some of this bluish or orange hue can enhance the "fire" of a diamond and is accepted without deleterious effect on the value of the diamond. But this stone has none, making it pretty much a non-factor.

While international diamond organizations are trying to standardize all laboratory certificates, that day still seems a way off. Some certificates provide more information than others, or use slightly different nomenclature.

Factors mentioned on the G.I.A. certificate and not the E.G.L. are:

Culet Size — The point at the very bottom of the diamond. Some cutters consider this a facet, others do not.

Symmetry — This refers to how well the overall angles and facets line up with each other. A well cut diamond should be almost perfectly symmetrical.

Crown Angles — Under the comment section, the G.I.A. sometimes makes mention of the Crown Angles. It does so only if the angles are 30 degrees or less, or 35 degrees or more.

Although grading is becoming more and more scientific, the certification process is still not 100 percent accurate. There is still an element of subjectivity involved. One lab might grade the same diamond slightly differently from another lab. Two gemologists in the same lab might also grade differently.

For diamonds of one carat and larger, I suggest using either the G.I.A. or HRD. The E.G.L. grades one-carat stones but the G.I.A. certificate is still preferred on larger stones. For stones smaller than a carat, the E.G.L. is by far and away the leading certifier.

The critical element is to get a certificate from a recognized, independent laboratory. It is of long-term tremendous importance for the sake of liquidity. Although you should never buy diamonds with the idea of quick resale, you should keep in mind the ultimate day when you may wish to liquidate. With an eye toward that day, you should regard the certificate like a pedigree or fingerprint representing your diamond. Trying to sell a diamond on the market with a certificate from an unknown or unacceptable lab is difficult, if not impossible.

Most importantly, you must insist on a certificate at the point of sale. Under very few circumstances is it wise for an investor to buy a loose unpapered diamond and then go about getting it certified himself. The dealer should provide a certificate at the point of sale.

But, even then, one must be careful. Having a certificate is not the end of being a wise and cautious buyer. Even assuming that the certificate is from a legitimate laboratory and not a counterfeit, there are precautions one should take.

Unfortunately, there have been some instances of stone switching by some dealers. You must be sure the diamond you receive goes with the certificate. A few firms have been known to repeatedly send a high quality stone to a legitimate lab, get a supply of top-notch certificates, and then attach those certificates to lower quality stones.

How do you guard against such "switching?" The E.G.L. (but not the G.I.A. oddly enough) encloses stones in a plastic pouch, sometimes with a microfilm copy of the certificate or a code number. This is meant to assure the client that the stone and the certificate match. This sealing protects the buyer and seller from the possibility of a switch by either party. Normally, guarantees of the stone's authenticity are voiced if the seal is broken. Many legitimate diamond investment firms in Europe (including some of the big French banks) send their diamonds in sealed plexiglas cubes.

This is all understandable from the legitimate dealer's point of view. He doesn't want the customer switching stones on him if the customer sends the stone back to the dealer for resale, for conceivably a person could take the diamond out, sell it, replace it with a synthetic zirconia or a lower quality diamond, and claim that the dealer has cheated him. At that point neither party has any recourse since it's the buyer's word against the seller's, and there can be no resolution of the claim.

I think the sealed cube is an indispensable tool of the honest broker and the conscientious investor alike. Once sealed, however, another problem faces the investor. How does he know the encapsulated stone matches the certificate? There are only two solutions here. Trust your dealer or get insurance.

If your dealer is reputable, and he seals the stone in a cube with his stamp, then he will guarantee that the stone and certificate match. If you're comfortable with his guarantee, and he's reputable, then you can sleep well. Alternatively, some firms offer an insurance policy guaranteeing that as long as the plastic case is unopened, the stone and certificate are the same.

In the absence of encapsulation, the best one can do — and it is only a second-best solution — is to demand from the seller a signed affidavit asserting that the stone he sold you is the same stone described on the accompanying certificate. If you have any doubts at that point, you may want to send the stone to the G.I.A. or E.G.L. to have that stone "re-verified" to be sure that the stone matches its certificate.

It is difficult for the average person, with no previous knowledge of diamonds or the diamond industry, to be sure of getting what he paid for. The larger point is that it is of paramount importance to have confidence in the integrity of whom you deal with. As the saying goes, "If you don't know your diamonds, know your diamond dealer."

7

Performance of Diamond Prices

Diamond prices are not easy to track.

Because they are not a fungible commodity, that is because they are not uniform and easily divisible like gold or silver, you can't cite any one price curve and say that it applies to all diamonds. Because of variations in size and quality, diamond prices do not move uniformly. Different grades and sizes move at different rates.

Still, it is important to say some general things about pricing and to give you as good an indication as possible of how diamond prices have performed, as well as how they might be expected to perform in the future.

PRICE HISTORY OF ROUGH DIAMONDS

First of all, we have to distinguish between rough prices and finished prices. Increases in prices at the rough stage are generally imposed from on high by DeBeers and not by the market, although naturally supply and demand factors must be carefully weighed by the cartel. DeBeers keeps a close eye on the premium being paid in the cutting centers for rough stones over and above DeBeers' prices. When that premium begins rising, DeBeers takes that as a signal that the market is ready for and can absorb an increase in the price for boxes of rough at the sight.

DeBeers' feeling is that if the market is willing to pay a premium for rough, then the "Syndicate" should get the benefit of those higher prices itself. So it raises prices. Anytime a premium of as much as 10 or 15 percent over the most recent DeBeers selling price is being paid consistently in the market for rough stones, one can pretty much count on another price increase by DeBeers.

Diamond prices prior to World War II are sketchy at best, particularly for cut diamonds. But a book by Percy A. Wagner published in South Africa in 1914, *The Diamond Fields of South Africa,* does give a glimpse of prices per carat of rough stone in the pre-Syndicate days during the period 1889 through 1913. The prices are in shillings per carat, and it is difficult to translate this into today's dollars. Nevertheless, we can see trends from these pricing figures.

In 1889, rough stones were selling, according to Wagner, at the rate of 19 shillings per carat. By 1913, they were selling for 67 shillings per carat — an increase of some 250 percent. There were, however, considerable fluctuations in the interim. In 1907, for example, the price had fallen to 64 shillings, but two years later, due to the Panic of 1907 presumably, it was back down to 47 shillings.

From 1913 through 1926, diamond prices were fairly steady. In 1926, according to Godehard Lenzon's *History of Diamond Production and the Diamond Trade*, rough diamonds were still selling for only 69 shillings per carat. A sharp drop to a little over 55 shillings followed in 1927, before climbing back up to 80.67 on the eve of the Great Crash of 1929. Thereafter, the price fell to 35.08 in 1932. Of course, this was mild compared to what happened to the Dow Jones Industrial Average and all other prices in that time period. Part of the decline, you recall, was also due to the emergence of vast new sources of supply in the late 1920s. At any rate, it was about this time that the newly formed worldwide marketing mechanism of the DeBeers cartel really took hold. It stabilized prices through the rest of the decade. And following World War II, diamonds started their inexorable modern-day climb.

Since the DeBeers arrangement of centralized marketing by the Central Selling Organization (CSO) in the Thirties, there has never been a decline in prices from DeBeers. That's quite a track record! **Figure 13** shows the record of rough stone price increases as mandated by DeBeers since 1948. It is a record of steadily rising prices and steadily growing rates of increase as we have entered the inflationary age. All told, it shows rough diamond prices have risen over 1,000 percent in the last 30 years.

Ultimately, rough stone pricing developments are a basis for cut diamond prices. That is only a partial explanation, however, for finished diamonds have enjoyed an even more impressive record of soaring prices than rough stones. But ultimately, price performance on both levels depends on available supply. From the point of view of the cutter, of course, he must not look only at his total costs (both material and labor), but also at demand, or what he thinks the market will bear.

Whether by intention or not, DeBeers has been able to create a condition of perpetual scarcity for the past 40 years. There are never more goods on the market than DeBeers believes the market can use at a given level of prices. So there is an actual scarcity, perhaps real, perhaps artificial, but a scarcity nonetheless. While the best estimates put diamond reserves on the decline, ultimately only DeBeers knows what's in the ground. And they're not talking.

The climate of scarcity is in part psychological too, a carefully inculcated image by DeBeers. DeBeers, through its tight management of rough diamond flows (and when necessary even finished diamond supplies) has instilled a fervent confi-

Figure 13.
DeBeers Rough Diamond
Price Increases Since 1948

Month	Year	% Increase	Compound % Increase
		1948 Base Year	100.00
September	1949	25.00%	125.00
March	1951	15.00%	143.75
September	1952	2.30%	147.06
January	1954	2.00%	150.00
January	1955	2.50%	153.75
January	1957	5.70%	162.51
May	1960	2.50%	166.57
March	1963	5.00%	174.90
February	1964	10.00%	192.39
August	1966	7.50%	206.82
November	1967	16.60%	241.30
September	1968	2.50%	247.33
July	1969	4.00%	257.23
November	1971	5.00%	270.09
January	1972	5.40%	284.67
September	1972	6.00%	301.75
February	1973	11.00%	334.94
March	1973	7.00%	358.38
May	1973	10.00%	394.23
August	1973	10.20%	434.44
December	1974	1.50%	440.95
January	1976	3.00%	454.17
September	1976	5.75%	480.29
March	1977	15.00%	552.33
December	1977	17.00%	646.23
August	1978	30.00%	840.09
September	1979	13.00%	949.30
February	**1980**	**12.00%**	**1,063.22**

Sources: International Diamond Annual, 1971 (covering 1949-69). Public Announcements, Diamond Trading Company (DeBeers) from 1971-1980.

dence among manufacturers, brokers, jewelers and retail customers, that diamonds are scarce and getting scarcer. Because of this solid feeling, holders of diamonds at all levels are able to feel confident about the current and future value of their diamonds.

PRICE HISTORY OF FINISHED DIAMONDS

The prices of finished diamonds are a different, though closely related, story. On the average, the general trend has been up at an even greater rate than rough, over 2,000 percent for some of the top grades, but again the rise has not been uniform. Larger, rarer, more perfect stones have risen at a much faster rate than stones of lesser size and quality — just as the best quality art or antiques have risen faster than poorer quality items. There have been a few cases of temporary price weaknesses, often at times of recession or after a rapid run up in prices, but these slumps, more appropriately called "technical adjustments," have been short term in nature, and in any case, were only temporary interruptions in the overall, inexorable price climb of the last 30 years.

Since we are interested in investment grade diamonds, however, let's look at the price performance records of these finest stones.

Obtaining precise appreciation figures is difficult, to say the least. There is no Dow Jones Index of the diamond market. Pricing information has to be based on being able to compare the price history of similar stones. Unfortunately, few precise records were kept until about ten years ago. At that time, cutters began to accurately grade their diamonds and obtain "certificates," and since then we were therefore able to obtain better and more accurate records of price trends of the better quality stones.

A useful starting point is the price history of the top-of-the-line — the "D Flawless" — diamond. Thirty years ago (well before the widespread use of certificates), the very best one-carat diamond (roughly the equivalent of a "D Flawless") sold at wholesale for about $500. In 1969, that figure was around $2,000. Today, a "D Flawless" diamond wholesale, costs well over $60,000.

Figure 14 shows that investment grade diamonds have risen by almost 30 percent per year. The table is based on average pricing increases of well cut, one-carat stones, D-H in color, Flawless through VS_1 in clarity.

In a very recent study, the respected H.I. Hassenfeld showed that for every one percent increase in inflation since 1967, investment grade diamonds have risen 1.5 percent. And for every one percent rise in the real gross national product, diamonds have gone up three percent.

On average, while rough stones have risen 12 to 13 percent per year over the last ten years, cut and polished investment stones have risen around 25 percent per year. In the latter half of the Seventies both percentages are even higher, but especially for finished investment goods. Why?

Why, for that matter, do rough stones rise at a rate faster than either inflation or dollar depreciation? The answers are threefold: DeBeers, national scarcity, and increasing demand for diamonds, particularly those of higher quality.

DeBeers has a vested interest in prices continuing to rise. The cartel will not take a loss because of inflation or currency devaluation.

Although diamonds are sold and paid for in terms of dollars, DeBeers has its own gold clause. It can, if it wishes, demand payment in gold. One way or another, if the dollar's value diminishes in terms of other currencies, DeBeers is going to raise prices to cover the depreciation — even if it means changing its secret price formula.

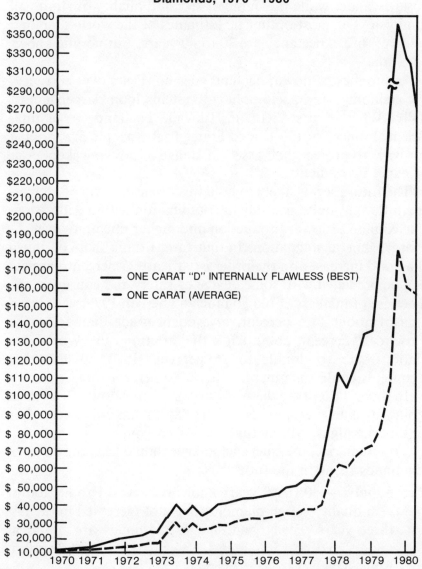

Figure 14.
Performance of $10,000 Invested
in Best and Average Gem-Quality
Diamonds, 1970 - 1980

Then too, we musn't forget the production factors. The costs of mining are tremendous and getting more so. And diamonds are getting scarcer at the same time. As the mines go deeper, costs escalate, while the number, size and quality of stones all diminish. The most optimistic estimates of the world diamond reserves' life expectancy are 30 to 40 years. But no one knows for sure.

As supplies go down, demand goes up. Fears over currency, the economy, and socio-political systems loom larger almost daily. Whether it's Vietnam, Taiwan, Thailand, Argentina, Brazil, France, or the United States itself, people are looking for ways to protect their assets in an age of growing skepticism of paper investments.

The future seems likely to hold in store a scenario of increasing inflation, quite possibly in combination with a depression-like climate of lower production and higher unemployment — that is, general stagnation. In that case, I think that continued diamond increases on the order of at least 25 percent per year can be predicted with some degree of safety and conservatism. The rate of increase could go much higher. In 1979, with inflation of about 13.5 percent, investment grade diamonds rose close to 50 percent, about triple the inflation rate. What if inflation were to double to 26 percent? It is possible that diamonds could then increase to an 80 percent rate.

In short, I don't see diamond prices coming down. I see them going up at an ever sharper rate. Today's diamond prices, while at all-time highs, will be tomorrow's bargains.

To summarize, the chief factors that should keep the prices of diamonds rising in the future are:

1. **Supply** — 30 to 40 years known reserves. Production of gem-quality rough diamonds has not increased in the last three years. Fewer and smaller diamonds are found as miners go deeper into mines. New discoveries, while promising, have yet to be proven.

2. **Demand** — Increasing enormously, especially as investing in diamonds is increasingly accepted on a worldwide scale. As investors seek alternative investments out of paper, diamonds will be a main beneficiary.

3. **DeBeers** — traditional role as regulator of market. Financially sound, it appears to be getting even stronger.

This rosy picture doesn't mean, of course, that you shouldn't be circumspect when buying diamonds. There are many pitfalls that face the unsuspecting investor.

8

Purchasing Your Diamond —
What, Where, and How to Buy

Now that we've discussed the production, distribution, grading and price performance of diamonds, you should have enough background information to consider making your first investment diamond transaction.

But what do you buy? From whom you buy? How do you go about making a purchase intelligently and securely? And, how much should you invest in diamonds.

HOW MANY DIAMONDS IN YOUR PORTFOLIO?

I have clients who feel that severe economic dislocation and readjustment is just around the corner. I have European and South American investors who have lived through double-digit inflation, social upheaval, political unrest and the like. People like these sometimes have as much as 50 percent of their portfolios in diamonds.

Given the economic, social, and political climate in the United States, it would not be imprudent to have 10 to 20 percent of one's overall investment portfolio in diamonds, however, you should have a minimum overall net worth of $50,000, excluding your home. While we don't have South American-style inflation — yet — and serious social and economic swings — yet — the signs are growing that these undesirable trends may become a possibility in the future. The prudent investor, therefore, must begin diversifying his assets to protect against these possibilities. If inflation increases, if America's fundamental economic situation worsens, then the amount of diamonds in your portfolio may have to rise.

As a rule of thumb, I would recommend that an investor have 20 to 30 percent of his overall portfolio invested in "hard assets." This should be broken down into silver (bags of "junk" coins and bullion), gold (Kruggerand and bullion), and diamonds — about one-third each.

The amounts of money you should place into diamonds and other tangibles depends, naturally, on your individual situation. Retired persons, for example, will probably be more concerned with income than long-term capital gains, so they may want to have a smaller percentage in diamonds. On the other hand, given the precarious position of Social Security and private pensions, retirees may do well to have a few diamonds as a hedge against collapse of the paper-backed pension system.

Diamonds are an ideal asset for long-term capital growth, and as such, are well suited for pension planning. Investors doing such planning should strongly consider diamonds. Changes under the ERISA rules now make it easy to include diamonds in pension and profit-sharing programs.

Diamonds would also be an excellent place to invest funds earmarked for your children's education, provided, of course, that they are still young.

WHAT TO BUY

As for what type of stone to buy, I refer you back to our previous chapters on the "Four C's" and on the "Fifth C" of certification. No matter what size stone you're buying, it's important to get the highest quality you can afford. And I recommend sacrificing a certain amount of weight in order to get a higher quality stone. Do not sacrifice grading standards in order to get a bigger diamond.

To summarize my earlier recommendations, try to stay within the top grades of color, which are "D" through "H" (or "1 + " through "2" on the E.G.L. Scale). In size, stay between 0.50 carat and 1.50 carats. Stones larger than 1.50 carats I recommend only for large diamond portfolios. Stick to the higher clarity grades, basically "Flawless" through "VS$_1$." And buy only round, brilliant stones that are unmounted and that fall within the range of acceptable proportions that we covered in Chapter 5.

These suggestions will probably change as supplies become more scarce and as demand increases. Ten years ago, for example, some advisers would have told you to buy only "D," "Flawless" stones. But now it is virtually impossible to buy a "D," "Flawless."So even the most conservative advisers now recommend a minimum "D" through "F" color range.

In fact, supply may become the operative factor in determining what to buy. As this is being written (early 1980) the supply situation is worsening. Dealers are happy to get any "certificated goods." Cutters are starting to allocate production to their best customers, and not taking on new clients.

Within the coming months I may have to begin, once again, expanding the parameters for "investment-quality" goods to include "I" and "J" colors and "VS$_2$" clarity. After all, what good is recommending a "G, VVS$_2$" if there are none available?

It is abundantly clear that all fine, certificated diamonds will continue to appreciate in value. Whether you purchase a one-carat "D," "Flawless" or a .50-carat "H," "VVS$_2$" they should both appreciate faster than inflation. My basic rule, however, still holds: buy the best available diamonds within your price range.

My approach has always been to buy quality, so I recommend that the modest investor go to a smaller size. Buying a three-quarter-carat or a half-carat stone, which have come into growing demand and acceptance and are highly liquid, is preferable to buying a poor quality, one-carat stone.

Quality aside, the question of size is very important. It involves a trade-off between appreciation and liquidity. These are the two big considerations in devising a diamond portfolio, even if it is a portfolio of just one stone. You must decide whether appreciation or liquidity (the ease of sale) is your first priority.

Generally speaking, the larger, more expensive stones have appreciated somewhat more than the smaller stones. At the same time, however, these stones are usually more difficult and time-consuming to liquidate. So this must be taken into consideration. And don't forget, you can't cut a diamond in half. If you have a $30,000 diamond, and you suddenly need $15,000 for some purpose, you can't sell half the diamond.

The investor must ask himself what his goals are and what his cash needs are likely to be in the future. Generally, the diamond investor settles on a combination of the two priorities of liquidity and long-term appreciation. There is no easy way out of the dilemma I just mentioned. Anyone investing in diamonds must simply realize that a stone of any size will require some care and patience to resell at a reasonable price.

Given an understanding of these choices, let me suggest a few sample portfolios for various levels of assets.

SAMPLE PORTFOLIOS

Let's say a person has $25,000 he wishes to invest in diamonds. I would suggest buying one good, full carat stone for $10-15,000 and two three-quarter-carat stones for $5,000 each.

For a $50,000 portfolio, I would suggest splitting it among one very fine large stone of one carat for around $25,000, another one-carat stone for $10-15,000, and a few smaller stones of a half- or three-quarter-carats, ranging from $3-6,000 each. For a portfolio over $100,000, I would suggest buying some of the larger, rarer stones, on the assumption that the purchaser has a good deal of money and isn't concerned if it takes two, three, or even four months to liquidate.

I know of one major European bank that is buying diamonds for its more substantial clients, and it will only buy one- to three-carat, "D" or "E", "Flawless" stones. That involves a lot of money, but these are clients who are buying for the long-term and who are aware of the more difficult liquidation situation of larger stones. It is obvious that it is going to take a while to find someone who is willing to spend $75-100,000 for a single stone.

WHERE TO BUY

The question of *what* to buy is not answered, however, by simply recommending sizes and grades. When you buy a diamond you also buy or should buy a diamond program. That is to say, you are buying the seller's reputation, his counsel and possibly assistance when you sell and, above all, his assurance of the diamond's quality.

You have a limited choice of sources from which to buy diamonds. Those sources are: jewelers, auctions and estate sales, banks (primarily foreign at this time), and investment diamond dealers. The average investor cannot hope to deal directly with a cutter.

A few jewelers have made an effort to sell what they call "investment diamonds." This is not the best avenue for purchasing the kind of stones we've been talking about for a number of reasons. First, they are not likely to have the rare, expensive, unmounted stones that are considered suitable for investment. The vast majority of jewelers are unlikely to have even a single, certified, investment-grade diamond in inventory. A few adventuresome jewelers are cautiously trying to enter the field, but with limited success. Their high overheads, as well as the fact that they are almost always far-removed from the primary sources of supply (the cutters), do not permit them to gear their prices to an investment level. The major problem, however, in purchasing from a jeweler is that they are likely to be of little help in reselling your diamond at a good price.

Although there are a few U.S. banks that will act as a fiduciary for diamonds held in Keogh accounts and the like, no bank in America will buy or sell diamonds for clients. There are substantial numbers of European banks who do so: Rothschild Bank, Societe Generale, Banque Suez (all in France). Many of the Swiss and German banks also deal in diamonds. For someone with an account at a foreign bank, it would be worthwhile to inquire about their diamond purchasing plans and check their prices. You should be willing, however, to store your diamond abroad in a bank's vault if you buy from this source.

Buying at auction is an attractive method of purchase. Often you can purchase diamonds at very reasonable prices, but it may pit you against professional bidders who are apt to have greater knowledge about the goods on offer. Remember the auction house's commission when calculating the final price. The buyer and seller each pay 10 percent, for a total of 20 percent. Auction houses, such as Christie's and Sotheby Parke Bernet in New York, are a viable outlet for buying and selling diamonds. They have regular jewelry auctions nearly every month. Sales of estate diamonds, usually handled by brokers, are also a possibility, but should probably be avoided unless you have gained some expertise in diamonds. These diamonds are almost always mounted in jewelry, and so the price will include the value of the setting as well as the broker's commission. And, with a mounting, it will be difficult to ascertain the quality of what you're buying. What's more, estate diamonds are not certified, so you are only guessing at what you've purchased. But if you really know what you're doing, you can probably get the best buys at estate sales. Be sure you buy at a genuine estate sale, not just an advertising come-on used by a jewelry store to sell some old inventory.

Probably the best source of investment diamonds are the legitimate investment diamond dealers. They are oriented toward the investor and usually have a complete program of services, usually including a viable resale or rebrokering facility. There are probably well over 100 in the United States, running the gamut from fly-by-night, fast-buck operators to honest, competent brokers. Unfortunately, the industry has attracted a fair share of bad apples. A few companies are overtly fraudulent, although they tend not to stay around for long. More are amateurish "bucket shops" that either sell low-quality stones with inadequate or misleading documentation for more than they are worth, or that sell the genuine item at outrageous prices. And there are, finally, a growing number of companies that sell good quality stones with expertise, integrity, and fair pricing.

How do you choose a legitimate diamond dealer? The first step is to get as much information as possible. That will be no problem. The pages of business newspapers, magazines, and newsletters are full of the advertisements of investment diamond dealers. Write to a number of them and ask for information. After reading as much as possible about the various companies you have under consideration, try to check out their reputation even further. Call their bankers. Are there any complaints? How long have they been in business? Generally, the longer a firm is in business, the more assurance you have of their integrity. How are they listed by Dun & Bradstreet? What does the Better Business Bureau in both your state and in the state where the firm resides say about them? Has the Attorney General or other agency in the state where the firm is based taken action against it? Are they registered with any government agencies? Remember, in diamonds, the first and most important decision you will ever make is selecting a dealer. He must have integrity, credibility, and a track record — and above all, you must feel comfortable with him.

Next, be sure that any company or jeweler you are considering buying diamonds from supplies a certificate of the diamond's grade from one of the recognized laboratories mentioned earlier. If the firm promises you a certificate from a lab you've never heard of, or if it assures you that the diamond has been graded "according to the standards of the G.I.A." or by "G.I.A.-trained gemologists," have nothing further to do with that firm.

Beyond that, find out what guarantees the firm provides that the stone and the certificate accompanying it are one and the same. In other words, that no switching has occurred. And, under what circumstances will they refund your money?

Buy-back guarantees, unfortunately, are often not usually promises to repurchase your diamond at some future date at a profit, as sound and reassuring as they appear. Whether selling diamonds or any other investment commodity, no legitimate investment firm should make warranties about future appreciation. There are risks in any investment. The most a reputable broker of any investment item can do is to use his "best efforts" to help you resell. The Securities and Exchange Commission has extremely strong views on any representations to the contrary. And while the SEC does not have any regulations affecting the diamond investment industry, most respectable diamond firms try to conform to the spirit of SEC regulations.

Beware too of high-pressure sales techniques, of frequent telephone calls from fast-talking salesmen making phenomenal price predictions and making promises of fast profit.

If you can, you should visit some of the dealers you are considering buying from. But don't be under any illusions about being able personally to judge the quality and value of a diamond, unless you are prepared to devote considerable time and effort to acquiring the knowledge of a gemologist.

I must caution the layman that to examine diamonds is a bit like a child with a telescope examining the surface of the moon. Gemologists study for years the art of diamond grading and examination. I can put down ten diamonds and ten cubic zirconia in front of the most sophisticated layman, and he will not be able to tell me which is which. And I could put down five "Flawless" and five "VVS_1" stones in front of a layman, tell him where the flaws are, and he can look at them under a 10-power microscope, and the odds are overwhelming against his being able to tell which ones are "Flawless" and which "VVS_1.

My experience has been that when people are encouraged to look at diamonds, often some sort of deception is involved. Perhaps, for example, hidden blue lights are used to enhance color. So long as the investor obtains a certificate from a recognized laboratory, and so long as he is confident that the certificate and his diamond are the same, there is little point in his using microscope, micrometer, and scale in the probably futile effort to examine the diamond himself.

PRICING

Attempting to get the best possible price is sensible, but it shouldn't become an end in itself. Price comparisons in diamonds are extremely tricky. "Bait and switch" is a common tactic. The buyer may get a certain price for a given grade of diamond from Firm A and call up rival Firm B to ask what their price would be for the same type of stone. The buyer may be told by Firm B, "We can get that one for 15 percent less." But then, adds Firm B, "Now, we don't happen to have that one in stock, but one we do have is . . . " And the price of the other stone is not so good as you've been led to believe.

Comparing prices is a difficult problem. There are no reliable listings of diamonds as there are for stocks and commodities. There are too many variables involved. As you've already learned, one "F," "VVS$_1$ diamond is not the same as another "F," "VVS$_1$" diamond because of the different cut characteristics, because of certification discrepancies and so forth. Two stones of exactly the same weight, color, and clarity could differ in price by as much as 25 percent because of poor cutting.

Diamond prices just are not as straightforward and predictable as, for instance, gold prices, because diamonds are a much more complicated commodity than gold. All of the big cutters have four or five different price levels. The essence of the pricing structure on New York's 47th Street is in negotiation. Who you know, and how long you've known him, is as important a consideration as anything else. The terms of payment also go into determining the price as does the volume of sales. Even the time of month is a factor. I know one cutter, for instance, whose prices are 10 to 15 percent higher at the beginning of the month than at the end of the month, because, at the end of the month, he's anxious to pay off his bank note.

Then too — it's all too easy to quote a list of prices on diamonds that you don't have and therefore can't sell. If a dealer you're attempting to buy from can't deliver the particular stone you want, then his attractive prices in the final analysis aren't so attractive after all.

There is a story that is told in New York's diamond district about a man who goes into the butcher shop to buy a pound of steak. He asks the butcher how much his steak costs. And the butcher replies, "It's $3.99 a pound." And the shopper exclaims, "But I can buy the same steak down the street for $1.99!" And the butcher asks him, "Well, why didn't you buy it down the street?" "The other butcher was out of it," the shopper answers. And the butcher tells him, "Well, if I was out of it, I would be selling it for $1.99, too." Unfortunately, the lesson is often the same in the diamond business.

So, while price is important, the investor should beware of becoming all-consumed by chasing for that furtive phantom, the absolute, rock bottom, "wholesale price." Pricing has to be examined in the light of the overall program and services offered by your prospective dealer. There are many services worth paying for, especially a strong and demonstrable resale ability, as well as guarantees against switching, proper certification, etc. Many diamond investors have, regrettably, found that the supposed "below wholesale" bargain turned out to be the worst deal in the long run.

But, just how can you check prices? Let's assume you are considering two diamonds. You must be sure you're comparing "apples and apples" (a difference of just one grade can mean a difference in price of as much as 20 percent). The color and clarity grade must be precisely the same. The diamonds must be within the same size range relative to "break points" (see Chapter 5). For example, two diamonds of exactly the same color and clarity could differ in price by 25 percent, if one were 1.00 carat and the other 0.97 carat. The two diamonds in comparison must be graded by the same laboratory. (Two diamonds, exactly the same in color, clarity, size, and cut, would legitimately be 15 percent apart in price if one had a certificate from a less acceptable lab.) The two diamonds must be cut within a narrow range of international tolerances with respect to proportions. For example, two otherwise similar diamonds could differ in price by 25 percent if one were poorly cut.

Once you're sure you're comparing similar diamonds, then

get copies of the certificates. After you've done that, then you can begin comparing prices.

If you feel you have enough information to make a valid price comparison, then examine the price in relation to the package of services offered by the competing dealers. You may find one dealer is more costly but has services worth paying for — such as an insurance guarantee of authenticity, a demonstrated proficiency at rebrokering stones at favorable commissions, trained gemologists, and good sources of stones. Alternatively, the lower-priced dealer may have an adequate program. If you can establish the same kind of trusting relationship you might have with a reliable stock broker, you'll do better in the long run.

To sum up the complicated issue of price: pricing is a very important consideration in buying — but it is only one of a number of equally important considerations. Comparison shopping is difficult because of the many components that go into the determination of each diamond, and every diamond is different — like different paintings all by the same artist. There are no daily listings of diamond prices. You should definitely try to compare prices, but be sure your comparisons are valid — an unscrupulous dealer can vary just one of the critical factors and the entire comparison will be invalid. After you have arrived at a true comparison, then examine the price in light of all the programs and services offered by your prospective dealer.

If you use the information in this book, if you approach choosing a dealer intelligently, if you ask polite but firm questions, and if you demonstrate a good grasp of the precise diamond qualities that you want in your investment, then you are unlikely to be cheated.

After forming a good idea of what stones are available in your affordable price range, then you should be able to approach a dealer with a specific objective of what size and grade stone you want. Again, try to get the best stone you can within your price range. Don't allow the dealer to tell you what you should buy or persuade you to switch away from your basic objectives. Naturally, there will be times when a dealer simply does not have the stones you're interested in, and you may have to compromise, but it still helps to have an objective in mind, to know what you want, and to approach the transaction with self-confidence.

STORING AND WEARING YOUR DIAMONDS

When you settle on a dealer and on a stone, pay cash and take possession. If the diamond is sent to you, make sure it is insured and sent by registered mail. Store it in a vault. For those not comfortable with bank safety deposit boxes, there are a number of private safekeeping depositories around. In his excellent *Complete Guide to Financial Privacy* (Alexandria House: 901 North Washington Street, Alexandria, Virginia 22314, $14.95), Mark Skousen lists a number of such non-bank vaults. (See appendix.)

It's also possible to wear and enjoy your diamonds. Many people decide to have their diamonds mounted in a fine jewelry setting. There are, of course, some precautions to take.

To begin with, I don't suggest you leave your diamond with a jeweler. It's not that he doesn't have an excellent reputation, but why tempt fate? Switching, unfortunately, can be a problem. It is possible that your diamond could be substituted for one three or four grades lower, and you might not be able to tell the difference. Find the oldest and best known jeweler in your town. Have him design or buy a setting for you. This can be done without your stone (if he insists on needing your stone to make the setting, have him buy a synthetic of the same size to work with). When the setting is ready, bring the stone in to be mounted. It shouldn't take more than one-half hour, unless it is a complicated and intricate piece of jewelry. You should stay and watch the mounting of the stone.

Once you have the ring or pendant, have the piece insured for your purchase price. In most cases you can get the piece covered under your homeowner's policy. From time to time you may want to have the stone appraised and increase your insurance coverage. A good investment diamond dealer can advise and assist you.

If you have your diamond mounted in a ring, you should try to avoid hitting the stone against hard surfaces. While it is true that diamonds are the hardest substance, they are also brittle, and can chip, especially around the girdle (outer edge). In the event you do chip your diamond, it can be recut. Unfortunately, you'll probably lose five to ten percent of the weight.

Do take adequate safety precautions. Diamonds are like cash. If one is stolen, it generally disappears and is never found. The international market is very fluid, and a diamond stolen in the United States today will probably surface next week in the Zurich or Hong Kong market.

If, in the future, you decide to sell the diamond that was mounted, you can do so easily. Naturally, you will have kept the original certificate in a safe place. Any jeweler can remove the stone from the setting, then deliver it plus the certificate to a dealer and agree on a price. As long as the stone matches the certificate you can make a deal. The value of the stone has not diminished because it was used in jewelry (provided, of course, it wasn't damaged).

The eventual resale of your diamond is another topic, with its own set of guidelines and precautions. That is the subject of the next chapter.

9

Liquidity: When Do You Sell and Where

Before you decide to go out and buy diamonds, a couple of caveats are in order.

First of all, diamonds (unlike shares in diamond mines) do not produce any interest or dividend income. And second, whatever their other advantages over stocks and bonds may be, diamonds do not have the instant liquidity of those more orthodox investment vehicles.

There is a real, viable market for reselling diamonds — but because it is relatively thin (compared to stocks or commodities), a quick, forced sale will fetch a lower price than a slow, patient attempt. The New York and Antwerp diamond districts are auction markets in the truest sense of the word. Astute buyers are quick to feel the urgency of a sale and will price their bid accordingly.

Much like art, antiques, and real estate, there is no instant market for diamond investors. That situation is rapidly improving, but there are still no daily quotes in the newspapers, for instance, and the informal bid-ask spread (the difference between the price at which you buy and the price you could get if you immediately resold the diamond) is still considerable.

The "spread" is narrowing as the market for diamonds becomes broader, as the investing public becomes more sophisticated, and as investment diamond dealers try to serve that market. Nevertheless, the disparity between the investor's buying and selling price is still wide enough that an investment diamond probably needs to be held at least a year after purchase to break even.

The critical factor in liquidity is time. It is not hard to sell a diamond — but you need adequate time in order to realize a good price.

As a general rule, a person should be prepared to hold onto diamonds at least three to five years after purchase to see good profits. Because of the bid-ask spread, and the amount of time necessary to liquidate, diamonds should not be considered as a "trading" vehicle. An investor should be prepared to allow anywhere from four to eight weeks to liquidate his diamond. If you are unable to wait this long, or if you are afraid you may have sudden need for the cash you have tied up in diamonds, then diamonds probably are not for you. Or perhaps you should be thinking of a smaller position in diamonds. Diamonds are meant for that portion of your portfolio which is designated for intermediate to long-term positions.

An important "if," when it comes to selling, goes back to our guidelines for buying. And that is: You will have no trouble selling your diamond if it was purchased with a certificate from a recognized laboratory. Diamonds with certificates from unknown or unaccepted laboratories are far more difficult to sell. Without a recognizable certificate, you run the risk of having your stone under-graded and under-appraised. The best you can do in that instance before you attempt to sell is to get the stone recertified by one of the major laboratories.

No matter which method you choose to sell your diamonds, it will be necessary for you to ascertain what the going price is. At the least, review what the recent history of rough price increases has been. Beyond that, you can get the most recent inventory price lists from dealers, or you can call them up and ask them how much they are charging for such and such a diamond. Allowing for their mark-up you can get a rough idea of what price you should be able to get for your stone.

There are a number of ways to sell diamonds. None of them is perfect. I believe that we will see major improvements in the public's access to the trade diamond bourses in the years to come, but for now, that access is limited. Participation on the diamond exchanges or bourses in New York and other diamond centers is not open to the public.

Nevertheless, there are a number of alternative ways to sell your diamonds, which are listed below in the rough ascending order of their importance and merits:

First, there is the do-it-yourself approach. Some people have had success in retailing their diamonds themselves. After getting an idea of what diamonds of the type and grade you own are selling for, you can advertise your diamond for sale in the classified section of a major newspaper, for instance the *New York Times*, *Wall Street Journal* or *Los Angeles Times*. On any Sunday you will see numerous ads in newspapers from private parties attempting to sell their diamonds. This may be time-consuming, but you can probably get a better price by selling to another individual than in any other way.

Jewelry stores are another possibility, but you will have to take some time to price-shop. Naturally, a jeweler will try to obtain the best price he can. He may offer you 10 to 30 percent or more below his wholesale buying price. A jeweler is only apt to buy from you if he thinks he can get a better deal than he can get from his supplier.

Still, if you walk into a reputable jewelry store, know what you're about and have a good quality diamond with a good quality certificate to back it up, you can get a relatively fair price. Again, know your price objective, which will take a little market research. Then, make the rounds of as many stores as possible and get as many offers as you can.

One of the easiest ways to sell your diamonds is at auction.

The two major auction houses are Sotheby Parke Bernet and Christie's. There are perhaps a dozen good secondary auction houses nationwide. In the auction season preceding the writing of this book, Sotheby Parke Bernet alone reported jewelry sales of close to $50 million from 45 auctions held internationally. The firm has jewelry auctions monthly in New York, one a year in Palm Beach, Florida, as well as others in Switzerland, Hong Kong, and England. The auction houses are emerging as a major factor in the resale market.

The advantage of selling at auction is that your diamond is simultaneously offered to an array of well-heeled buyers. If you have a good quality diamond, bidding can be vigorous, and your diamond may yield a high price — somewhere between "wholesale" and "retail." You can put a reserve, or floor price on the stone, below which the auction house is not authorized to go. Thus you can be assured of a minimum price. Your diamond will have been taken on consignment by the auction house, which then sends lists of its merchandise for sale to potential buyers around the world. Even a single diamond can be handled on consignment by one of these houses.

The commissions at auction are generally around 20 percent. Usually, the auction house's commission is split evenly between the buyer and seller, say ten percent of the final price to each party. The major, reputable auction houses also furnish reliable appraisal services for jewelry and papered diamonds.

Finally, you can have the stone brokered. Most reputable investment diamond companies are willing to broker stones, both for clients and non-clients. Of course, a company will usually accord preferential treatment to those to whom it has sold diamonds. Increasingly, also, there are more traditional diamond firms, with membership on one of the diamond exchanges, that are willing to broker stones for the public at the exchange. Their fees for this service range from five to 20 percent.

The best approach is, if possible, to resell the stone through the firm you bought it from — assuming it is a reputable company. The investment diamond firm can do one of three things. He may wish to buy the stone for his own inventory if he needs such a stone. He can sell it for you through a broker with membership on a diamond bourse. Or, he can take it on consignment, list it in his inventory, and try to sell it at current prices. A typical commission would be ten percent for that service.

The simplest lucrative avenue is probably to place your diamond on consignment with the firm from which you bought it. If you go to another firm, that firm is apt to try to buy the stone back at as low a price as it can — below what it would pay its supplier. If the stone is brokered on one of the exchanges, it will bring a "sub-wholesale" price. But if it can be sold as part of your original dealer's inventory at current prices, you are apt to net (after commission) a better return.

If time is a factor, brokering through an exchange member or selling directly to a broker is faster, but you can expect to receive less. Whatever method you use, it is again wise to do a little research on prices in order to form a goal of what you realistically would hope to receive for your stone. And then shop around.

Your best protection, your best assurance of getting fair value at resale time, is to have a good quality stone, no matter what the size, with a good certificate.

When you leave a diamond on consignment with an investment diamond company or other broker (or auction house for that matter), it is prudent to take a few precautions. Get a signed receipt stating that the company has your specified grade of diamond on consignment. The receipt should also spell out the code number of the stone's grading certificate, the seller's commission, the length of time the stone is to be held in the firm's inventory and, if you wish, the minimum price you are willing to accept for the stone.

Another way of disposing of diamonds, without actually selling them, is via the growing practice of barter, that is, exchanging your diamond — either directly or through brokers — for something else you want. Non-monetary transactions are becoming increasingly popular as the value of money becomes unreliable and as the need for quiet and discreet transfers of wealth grows. And as this phenomenon spreads, taking in bigger and more important transactions, diamonds will come into increasing demand for the purpose. They are ideally suited. They are small and extremely portable, they are accepted worldwide, and their value can quickly be determined.

The advantage of barter to the owner of diamonds is that, often, he can get much greater value for his diamond than in any of the resale methods previously discussed.

Barter tends to take place at the retail value of the items being bartered. So a diamond holder wishing to trade for land, for instance, can maximize the value of his diamond in negotiating an exchange with the land owner. The problem, of course, is that if you have your eye on a particular piece of land, and that particular land owner doesn't care to have your particular diamond, no deal is apt to take place on that basis. (That's why money came into existence as a common medium of exchange.)

I believe that diamonds will increasingly acquire the functions of money — that it will come to be a much more recognizable medium of exchange. Like gold, it is a respected store of value. What's more, as standardized ways of measuring and comparing diamond values continue to evolve, diamonds will become easier to use in making larger transactions.

But for now, the problem can be solved by participating in one of the "barter exchanges" that are popping up all over the country. These are services or "clubs" that bring together — sometimes through the use of barter credits or vouchers — people offering or seeking different goods and services. It is estimated that there are 10 to 20 nationwide. Most of these are locally or regionally oriented.

While would-be diamond investors should be aware of the unique liquidity characteristics of diamonds, they should not be frightened by them. Again, the investor who buys a good quality stone from a reputable dealer, who provides a recognized certificate, should not have liquidity problems.

In fact, diamonds should become more and more liquid in the years ahead. Within the next few years, I expect to see the development of a secondary market of sorts, oriented toward diamond investors. There have already been a couple of ill-fated attempts at establishing a diamond "exchange" with public access that have failed, either because of the poor credentials of the organizers or because the efforts were simply premature. Nevertheless, I think the development of such a market, complete with daily price listings for certain grading categories, is inevitable. The growing number of diamond investors assures it, and the emergence of accepted and standardized methods of grading and certification makes it quite feasible.

In any event, you don't have to buy diamonds solely with the future promise of liquidity in mind. Even now, there is adequate liquidity for the patient, prudent investor. A market very definitely exists. Though the public does not have direct access to it in all its aspects, the existence of the diamond bourses, the constant trading in streets and offices of the diamond centers, the network of investment dealers, and the regular auctions provide plenty of liquidity and leverage for the seller.

10

Diamonds and Taxes

The tax consequences of buying and selling diamonds, as may be expected, vary according to your own personal situation. In this chapter, I'll show the generally favorable tax treatment accorded to diamond ownership.

SALES AND/OR USE TAX

Many states have a sales and/or use tax. If you purchase the diamond from a dealer in the state or city where you reside, the sales tax will be added to the price of the stone. Most states, however, do not require merchants to collect sales tax on diamonds delivered out of state.

Some states, however, may require the buyer to remit the appropriate sales or use tax on diamonds purchased from an out-of-state vendor. In that case, the purchaser should inform the appropriate local tax office of the purchase and then pay the tax. If sales or use tax is paid, it is tax deductible against ordinary income.

ORDINARY INCOME TAX

Since diamonds yield no current income, there are no ordinary income tax implications. Interest paid on funds borrowed to purchase diamonds is tax deductible against ordinary income.

CAPITAL GAINS TAX

Diamonds sold at a gain are subject to capital gains tax. For tax reasons, diamonds should be held for an absolute minimum period of one year. In this way, you will be subject to long-term capital gains treatment (a maximum tax rate of 28 percent for the highest tax bracket persons). Long-term capital gains are taxed at 40 percent of income tax rate on ordinary income. If held for less than one year, you will pay your ordinary income tax rate on any gains achieved. (*N.B.* — as stated previously, diamonds should always be considered a long-term investment, three years at a minimum.)

Most purchasers of diamonds are reasonably sophisticated investors who fall within the top income tax brackets. Many are purchasing diamonds as a long-term hedge against inflation. Capital gains treatment is therefore highly desirable, as opposed to taxation at income tax rates. Comparisons between the after-tax return on diamonds (at capital gains rates), and Treasury Notes, for example, are illuminating.

Let's look at $10,000 invested in T-Notes:

$10,000 investment

15% return equals	$1,500
Less: approximate maximum tax rate on unearned income — 70%	1,050
Aftertax return	$ 450 (or 4½%)

Let's compare that to a $10,000 investment in diamonds. If

the appreciation was only 15% for the year, the same as T-Notes, the after-tax results are dramatically different.

$10,000 investment

15% return equals	$1,500
Less: maximum long term capital gains tax at 28%	420
Aftertax return	$1,080 (or 10.8%)

Investors in the higher rates of income tax should avoid income producing investments unless absolutely necessary. The tax consequences are obvious. Even for a 50 percent taxpayer, the after-tax dollars retained in the example would be startling: $1,200 for diamonds and only $750 for T-Notes. It should be noted that foreigners will generally not be taxed in the United States on diamond appreciation.

TAX-FREE EXCHANGE (BARTER)

Under SEC 1031, the IRS allows for a tax-free exchange of similar property held for investment purposes. Thus, it would appear that "trading-in" your diamond for a more expensive diamond would not be a taxable event. Capital gains tax would be payable later when a more expensive diamond was sold, unless of course, there was another trade-up to an even more expensive diamond. And one could continue to trade up without creating a taxable event.

DIAMOND TAX SHELTERS

During the last few years, there have been a number of

dubious gem tax shelters sold involving diamonds and other precious and semi-precious gems.

In very basic terms, the deal goes like this: the investor buys an expensive and often rare gemstone, often one whose value is not readily determinable (a very large, unusual diamond, or perhaps a rare, colored diamond). An appraiser is brought in who then gives an inflated value to the gem, often three to ten times the purchase price. The investor then donates the stone to a non-profit museum or school. The investor then takes a deduction for his "donation" at the appraised price. In the maximum income tax brackets there could be substantial income tax savings if the scheme held up before the IRS.

I believe that if all the facts are known, the plan will be found transparent, and that it would never hold up, and consequently I never recommend this kind of investment. The IRS recently disallowed one such tax shelter. The ruling stated that, although the promoter had assured the taxpayer the gems were worth three times what he had paid, the fair market value was cost, not exaggerated estimates. Check with your tax attorney. You can, of course, donate your diamonds to any charitable cause you like, but the deduction that you will be allowed for your donation will only be your "purchase price."

PENSION AND PROFIT SHARING PLAN, KEOGH AND IRA PROGRAMS

American banks have recently begun to enter the diamond picture via Keogh and pension plans and Keogh and IRA accounts. Thanks to recent clarification in the definition of the "prudent man rule" governing what types of investments are acceptable for pension plans, the door has been opened to diamonds and other collectibles. Because of what inflation has done to traditional investments, such as stocks, bonds, and savings certificates, things such as diamonds have come to be regarded as at least as prudent an investment as the somewhat tarnished old stand-bys.

The clincher came in early 1979, when the U.S. Labor Department ruled that the 1974 Employee Retirement Income Security Act (ERISA), which governs trust administrators and pension fund portfolio managers, does not preclude non-traditional types of investments by private pension plans. Already, the IRS had ruled that diamonds were acceptable for use in tax-deferring Keogh and Individual Retirement Account (IRA) accounts.

The advantages of diamonds in pension funds, trusts, and IRA or Keogh accounts are two-fold. One is their proven ability to outpace almost any other type of investment on a consistent, predictable basis. The second is their exemption from income taxes. These dual advantages were noted in a September 1978 article in the publication *Trusts & Estates:*

> . . . (I)n view of the unceasing rise in inflation and nominal tax rates, the existing tax structure requires investments other than taxable income-generating forms into assets from which income is taken "in kind" and capital gains are deferred, e.g. real estate and diamonds.

> . . .In other words, total investment management should incorporate diamonds, as well as real estate, mortgages, equity and debt instruments, in order to be responsive to major economic indicators and thereby giving rise to more predictable and stable investment objectives.

> . . . Investment quality diamonds do not produce income. Rather, such investment is for the long term to take advantage of capital appreciation. Consequently, investment-quality diamonds are a natural inclusion in a portfolio of long-range goals and preservation of assets in remainder-man trusts. The balance of the portfolio can be utilized to obtain income for the life tenant.

Corporate pension or profit sharing plans can often include diamonds easily; that is, with no change in the underlying trust document. If the trustees or investment committee have discretion in where to place the assets of the trust, then diamonds can be added easily. Some trust documents, especially ones written more than ten years ago, may specifically define where the trust may invest its assets and may allow investments in only a few narrowly restricted areas. In this case, the trust deed may have to be amended to broaden the areas of investment alternatives.

If your corporate or other pension plan does not invest in diamonds, you may wish to consider setting up your own supplementary plan with a bank as a fiduciary. If you qualify, the IRS allows an employee to set aside up to $1,500 (or 15 percent of income — whichever is less) tax-free income every year in an IRA. Or, if you are self-employed, you can set aside up to $7,500 (or 15 percent of income — whichever is less) annually tax-free in a Keogh Account. The big advantage of these types of retirement trusts is that they are self-directing, that is, *you* make the decision where to invest the funds. Not all banks have the facilities for self-directed Keogh and pension programs, but the number is rapidly increasing.

The advantages are considerable. Let's say you are in the 50 percent tax bracket, and you want to buy a $5,000 diamond. First, you have to earn $10,000 and pay 50 percent in taxes, which leaves you with $5,000 to buy the diamond. With an IRA or Keogh or pension plan account, however, you can buy with *before-tax* (or deferred tax) dollars. So, if you put $10,000 in one of these plans, you can purchase a *$10,000 diamond,* instead of a much smaller $5,000 diamond. And on top of that, all the accumulated gains that the diamond accrues over the years until your retirement are not subject to capital gains tax, much less to income tax. When you retire, and you close out the account and sell the diamond, you will have to pay tax based on the favorable ten-year averaging income formula on the value of the diamond distributed. But presumably, you will then be in a lower tax bracket. If you die before retirement, the value of the diamond will be estate tax-free for most estates, although ordinary income taxes must be paid.

It is important to choose a fiduciary (usually a bank trust department) that has acquired some knowledge and experience in dealing with diamonds. The appendix contains a partial list of trust companies that regularly place diamonds in their clients' IRA and Keogh accounts. Although the bank or trust company itself must purchase the diamond on your behalf, the new "self-directed" plans authorize the investor to instruct the bank as to what type of diamond to buy, who to buy it from, and at what price.

REPORTING REQUIREMENTS AND RECORD KEEPING

Currently, I know of no reporting requirements to any local, state, or federal agency. You are not required to give your social security number nor are you required to present identification when you make a diamond purchase. This could change, of course, but at present, there seems to be no attempt to require reporting of diamond transactions.

Any diamond vendor, of course, must keep normal business records, and those records could be subpoened or be subject to an IRS audit. While it is highly improbable that the IRS would subpoena the records of a jeweler or diamond merchant to see who purchased diamonds, the buyer who is concerned about the privacy of his transaction should be aware that he is not protected by any confidentiality restrictions.

Most diamond dealers will accept payment in cash, however, any cash payment will probably be deposited in a bank. Cash deposits of more than $10,000 must be reported by the bank to the IRS.

Since there are no reporting requirements, investors should keep careful records of their purchases and sales, since these figures will form the basis for tax treatment.

Naturally, all tax planning should be done in consultation with your personal tax advisor. Generalizations are just that. They may not apply to your own particular situation.

11

A Word About Precious Colored Gemstones: Rubies, Emeralds, and Sapphires

There may come a time when "colored stones" will be as good an investment as diamonds, but that time is not now. Rubies, sapphires, and emeralds have been promoted by some firms as equals of the diamond as an investment. Some even suggest that the more common or "semi-precious" stones (aquamarines, garnets, topaz, etc.) are good investments.

To be sure, colored stones do have their attraction. Their appreciation, in a few cases, has actually been better than that of diamonds. In the higher grades they are actually far more rare than diamonds. And too, the sources of colored stones are much less certain and secure even than diamonds, their much harder cousins — suggesting the possibility of dramatic price potentials for the future.

But these facts are insufficient to justify an investment in rubies, emeralds, or sapphires for the great majority of investors. Unless a person has special expertise or is willing to acquire it, I believe colored stones are far too speculative for the average investor. There are three main reasons for this.

First of all, while geological and political realities give them an ostensibly favorable supply-demand situation, colored stones lack an organization such as DeBeers to control their production and distribution. That means that supply and price of colored stones are unreliable and unpredictable, unlike the diamond market. Wide price swings are common. What's more, let's not forget the tremendous promotional job DeBeers has masterminded on the diamond dealer's behalf.

Secondly, and partly because of the foregoing, there is no organized resale market for colored stones as there is with diamonds. Even though the existing diamond exchanges are not accessible to the public, they do provide an indirect market and a reservoir of liquidity. Nothing of the kind exists for colored stones. Selling a colored gemstone back into the trade is extremely limited and highly unreliable.

The largest cause of this is the third and most important of our reasons why colored stones are too speculative for the average investor. As yet there is no widely accepted standardized set of grading rules, and hence no widely accepted certification for colored stones. Therefore, the investor is almost entirely dependent on the good faith of the seller of the stone — in my opinion an inappropriate way of buying any investment.

The American Gemological Laboratory (A.G.L.) has made some good efforts toward the grading and certification of colored gemstones. As this book is written, the A.G.L. is the only laboratory that issues certificates for colored stones. The E.G.L. is also working on a grading and certification program of its own, but it is significant to note that it will probably be a different system.

The point remains that, as yet, the grading of colored stones is nowhere near scientific or adequate enough to qualify them for investment. Whatever the merits of the A.G.L. or E.G.L. programs, these certificates are little used by the trade — a telling fact. As you may recall, it took years for the trade to accept G.I.A. diamond grading standards. So I think we can expect similar resistance in the instance of colored stones. We can also expect a period of years in which the grading standards will be changed and refined. In the meantime, the investor would be buying at a time of flux. So, unless he is an expert in colored stones, and he knows what he is buying, he must be willing not only to trust the integrity of the seller, but also to run the risk that the grade on his certificate may become obsolete three years from now.

This in turn impinges on the possibilities of dependable resale. Whereas transactions in diamonds can often be handled long distance on the basis of the diamond's G.I.A., HRD, or E.G.L. certificates, that is not now possible with colored stones.

When it comes time to liquidate the colored stone portfolio, the buyer is apt to find that he has little recourse but to go back to the company that sold it to him — if it's still in business. He may find that the certificate that was provided — if one was provided — makes no impression on other members of the gemstone industry.

He may find, indeed, that his ruby or emerald or sapphire was actually a piece of cut glass — or more likely, that the stone's color is not as deep and rich, not as near to the ideal true color, as he had been led to believe.

"Color" is a far more complicated grading factor in colored stones than in diamonds. Even the origins of two stones, though they may have the same apparent color, can make a big difference in price.

"Clarity" is equally tricky. Some experts say it is desirable to have some flaws in a stone, just to remove any doubts about a stone's authenticity or to prove where that particular stone came from. Is it a Thai ruby or a Burmese ruby? And so it goes. Not very reassuring, is it?

If you're still intrigued by colored stones and if you have sufficient wealth to afford a high-risk speculation, then at least take a few precautions. First of all, learn as much as you can about a particular type of stone that interests you. Read some of the more scientific literature available. Visit museums with gemstone collections. And then, before you buy, be very careful in selecting a dealer.

Then buy only the highest quality possible. That means the truest color of red or green possible (in the case of rubies and emeralds). Be extra careful to detect possible tricky lighting techniques. It is so easy to enhance a stone's color temporarily — sometimes by irradiation. And be sure that the stone is authentic. Either of the labs mentioned can at least tell you that. And, for what it's worth, insist on a certificate from one of those labs, with assurances that the stone and certificate match, if that's possible.

Better yet, wait a few years until this market has had a chance to mature a bit. Let colored stone grading and certification evolve a bit more and become more acceptable. You may miss some price action, but you could save yourself a lot of headaches and perhaps a lot of money.

12

The Future for Diamonds

As dramatic as the past price performance of diamonds has been, I believe that they are now on the threshold of even more explosive price behavior.

A major factor in future price expectations, of course, is dwindling supply. Regardless of the fate of the DeBeers cartel, production of diamonds is expected to diminish over time — although not in a straight line. From the current annual level of about 10 million carats of gem quality rough diamonds, production is expected to peak at between 15 and 16 million carats by the end of the century. In the first decade of the next century, production will begin falling off sharply until, by the year 2020, annual production peters out almost completely. This assumes no new, major discoveries.

What's more, the percentage of investment quality stones from any given level of production will diminish at an accelerating rate as years go by. Currently, it is estimated that less than 50,000 carats of cut, investment grade stones are recovered from the annual total of 45 million carats of rough. Using constant definitions of "investment grade material," there is little doubt that, by the end of the century, no more than 10,000 carats of new investment diamonds will be available to a hungry market each year. And thereafter the flow of new stones will likely diminish even further.

As a result, the definition of "investment quality" will broaden. People will come to accept more flawed, less colorless stones for investment purposes, with the result that higher grade stones purchased now will be considerably more valuable than past price extrapolations might lead us to expect. The future of DeBeers is of prime concern to all diamond investors, since its control has helped eliminate most of the volatility from the diamond markets. Present indications are that the company will offset its declining direct control of production with increased indirect control of distribution, not only of rough stones, but also of cut diamonds. DeBeers production from its own mines will diminish as a percentage of total world production, however, DeBeers will probably participate to a great extent in the world's most important mining ventures. And it should be able to maintain effective control of production through a perpetuation of its existing purchase and marketing agreements with the various world producers.

A collapse of cartel control into the volatility of the open market is improbable. It would certainly not be in the interest of the major producers to precipitate such a circumstance. The only producer with cartel-breaking potential would presently seem to be the Soviet Union, but self-interest dictates it do nothing to disrupt the record of price escalation.

It is quite possible that the Russians will seek a larger share of the profits from their diamond sales, and they may have to achieve this through their own separate marketing effort. At worse, this would simply lead to an "ologopoly" situation, instead of the present "monopoly" situation. In other words, there would be two major sellers, instead of the current one. The economics should not appreciably change, nor should price behavior.

Far more important than supply, though, I think, is the demand side of the equation. So let's take supply as a given for a moment, and let's make some assumptions about economic conditons over the next ten to twenty years.

It appears as if the present inflationary climate will be with us for some time. Inflation will probably accelerate during the coming years, punctuated by periodic recessions. In other words, contrary to the conflicting predictions of hyperinflation on the one hand and deflationary contraction on the other, I think this nation and the world will stumble along in a blue funk of deepening "stagflation."

Under these conditions, demand for diamonds as an alternative or hedge investment will soar. It is highly significant that the current levels of diamond prices, high as they seem to many, have been achieved with relatively small investor participation. There are probably no more than 25,000 diamond investors (as opposed to persons who buy lower quality diamonds for more traditional reasons).

Total investment diamond portfolios — and it would be impossible to make an exact estimate — pale into insignificance when compared to the dollar value of stock portfolios, money market funds, savings deposits, or even gold or silver investments. When people start fleeing in earnest from traditional paper dollar investments into hard assets, the base of diamond investors will balloon. A large shift out of stocks and savings, which is already happening to a small extent and which will come in a rush as inflation and dollar depreciation worsen, would cause diamond demand to expand manyfold.

Diamond investments will burgeon regardless of what happens to inflation. It will take a long time for stocks and bonds to recover the confidence of the investing public, such as they had in the sixties. The diamond price performance record — irrespective of inflationary forces — is very impressive. Diamonds present themselves as a reliable, blue chip investment.

Diamonds are coming of age as a practical investment vehicle just when the public is most ready for them. As shown, certification has made diamonds a more trustworthy, fungible, and liquid investment. The old barriers to their entry into pension funds and the like are falling. More and more banks and portfolio managers are accepting diamonds.

The investment diamond industry, while it has had a traumatic birth, is now established and has done much to popularize diamonds. The industry has propagated the certificate as a product warranty and as a marketing tool for both buyer and seller. And they have improved considerably the liquidity of the market.

With the development of a secondary market, which is imminent in the next three to four years, diamonds will have come full circle. They will have been made whole as an investment, and they will take their place along with other investment vehicles as a publicly traded and held asset. When this happens, when individual and institutional investors begin getting into diamonds in a big way, prices will rise inexorably.

In fact, they may rise so fast that it will take all of DeBeers' energy and ingenuity to restrain them. This may mean that, in the future, diamond prices will begin to behave more like some of their competitive investment vehicles — in cycles. That is, with higher price rises, we may have to accept some temporary price reversals. Nevertheless, for long-term investors, who take advantage of today's opportunities, that will be a small bother.

Within the context of the present market structure and the present level of participation, I expect minimum annual price increases for investment grade diamonds, of 25 percent a year. That might be taken as an average throughout the economic cycle — from inflationary peak to recessionary valley. During the more inflationary years diamonds could easily rise 40 to 50 percent per year.

Will there come a time when diamonds cease to be a good investment? One would be when the supply-demand situation is radically altered. If, for some reason, diamonds fell out of favor, if the traditional engagement ring want out of style, then demand for diamonds might fall off so badly that prices of investment grade diamonds would weaken. This is not very likely, however.

Another conceivable development might be the sudden discovery of vast new reserves of diamonds that DeBeers is not able to bring under its control. It's possible to conceive of the market being flooded with cheaper diamonds, undermining historical price levels, and even degrading the image of diamonds. This is possible, but extremely unlikely.

Finally, a major reversal of economic trends could alter demand for diamonds and change the course of diamond prices. That would be a deflationary scenario. Government would bring inflation under control, discontinue deficit spending, eliminate trade deficits, and return to honest money. Unfortunately that scenario also seems to be far off.

In the meantime, then, diamonds should be seriously considered and included in every sizable portfolio. The future for diamonds is very bright. Indeed, wise investors can reap handsome profits if they proceed intelligently, cautiously, and knowledgeably. Diamonds are coming of age as a viable investment alternative, and investors beginning now will be in an enviable position in the coming years.

Appendix

Guidelines For Buying Diamonds

Before you buy your first diamond, go through the following checklist of "do's" and "don'ts." It may save you some headaches and probably some money later.

1. **Don't buy diamonds unless you have an overall net worth, excluding your home, of at least $50,000.**
   Diamonds are for the fairly sophisticated investor of some means. You should have a reasonable knowledge of investments and markets before embarking on a diamond investment program. (See **Chapter 8**)

2. **Invest up to a maximum of 20% of your portfolio in diamonds.**
   And that's probably too much. Diamonds are for that portion of your portfolio that you can set aside for a long-term, slightly liquid commodity. Your portfolio should be well balanced in other areas. (See **Chapter 8**)

3. **You should plan to hold for at least 3 years, preferably longer given the limited liquidity, and the bid-ask spread.**
   Diamonds are definitely not a trading or speculative vehicle, but an intermediate to long-term investment" (See **Chapter 9**)

4. **Allow time to liquidate.**
   Plan on 6 to 8 weeks. It could take less, but if allowed plenty of time, you won't be disappointed if it should take longer. (See **Chapter 9**)

5. **Insist on a certificate from a recognized independent gemological laboratory. Accept no substitute.**

I recommend the G.I.A., E.G.L., or HRD. "G.I.A. standards" or a diamond graded by a "G.I.A.-trained gemologist" are simply not enough. You just can't be sure what you're really getting. A certificate from a little used or unknown laboratory will make it infinitely hard to sell your stone when the time comes. (See **Chapter 6**)

6. **Buy quality — the best you can afford.**

Sacrifice on size — not quality. I recommend between 0.48-1.50cts, D-H in color, IF-VS$_1$ in clarity, round brilliant shape, and cut to specific international tolerances. (See **Chapter 8**)

7. **Deal with a diamond specialist.**

There are many entrepreneurs in the field, most of whom know little about diamonds. Deal with someone who has expertise in the field, not someone who sold Florida land last year and London commodity options the year before. (See **Chapter 8**)

8. **Buy from a reputable dealer.**

I've saved this for last because its the most important. Check the references and recommendations of your dealer. See how long he has been in business. See if the dealer is registered with any governmental agency. Recently, the New York Attorney General's office required that diamond firms register with them. Thousands of investors have been victimized by the diamond frauds; others have made excellent investments. Don't you be the one to get ripped-off. Take your time and investigate your dealer. (See **Chapter 8**)

Rip-Offs To Avoid

1. Be wary of in-house certification (self-grading).

Again, always insist on a certificate from an independent gemological laboratory. Self-grading presents just too many potential conflicts of interest. If your dealer gives his own grading analysis, it is very tempting to overgrade by one or two categories. The layman can't tell and the dealer adds another 20 to 30 percent to his profit. The independent gemological laboratories do not sell diamonds and therefore have no interest in either upgrading or down-grading. (See **Chapter 6**)

2. Beware of appraisals.

Most appraisals (as opposed to laboratory grading certificates — which are not appraisals) are unrealistically high. The seller usually gets a high appraisal (from his friendly appraiser) then convinces you that you're getting a great "deal" when he sells you a stone at 25 percent below the appraisal price. (See **Chapter 8**).

3. Beware of bait and switch tactics.

a. Low Ball Pricing.

Company A, a legitimate diamond dealer, gives a price. Company B, not so honest, says he can sell you the same stone 15% cheaper. You discontinue talking to Company A and begin serious discussions with Company B. When you go to buy the actual stone, it turns out they just sold it, but have another "almost" as good. Often the investor takes the bait, and then gets switched. The second stone is usually a bad deal. Watch out! The difference in price between just one grade of color or clarity can be as much as 20%. Don't be switched. Insist on the original stone promised. (See **Chapter 8**)

b. No Inventory
In this one, the dealer makes up a fictitious stone and tries to get you to send money for it. When he gets your money, he tries to buy a diamond, any diamond, close to your original choice, and then convinces you to take it. Once he's got your money, it's hard to get it back. Don't send money unless you have a quote on a specific stone. Have the dealer send you a copy of the certification before you send any money. (See **Chapter 8**)

c. Switching into Color Stones
The company gets your name from one of dozens of lists and sends you a nice diamond brochure. After talking to a salesman, you're convinced that colored stones are the investment of the future. Don't be fooled. If you want diamonds, don't be talked into colored stones. (See **Chapter 11**)

4. Be suspicious of claims for shipment direct from a laboratory.
Switching can be a problem with any precious stone. You should try to get some guarantees from your dealer against this possibility. Ideally, shipment direct from a reputable laboratory would be perfect. Some firms claim that the labs are shipping on their behalf. The G.I.A. will not ship stones directly to clients on

behalf of a diamond investment company. On occasion, the E.G.L. will do it. If you are unsure, call the laboratory directly to confirm. (See **Chapter 6**)

5. Beware of dealers selling fancy cuts at round brilliant prices.

The fancy shapes (pear, emerald, marquise, etc.) generally sell well below the price of a round stone of precisely the same quality. For example, a pear-shaped diamond should sell for about 30% below the same quality round stone. Some companies sell fancy shapes at only a little bit below the price for round diamonds. I recommend purchasing only round brilliant diamonds for investment. (See **Chapter 8**)

6. Be dubious of guaranteed buy-backs.

No legitimate investment company, whether it's selling diamonds or commodities, can guarantee a buy-back. The most a reputable firm will do is use its "best efforts" to help you resell your diamonds. The SEC takes a dim view of such guarantees. You should, too, if anyone offers a "guaranteed" buy-back or profit. (See **Chapter 8**)

7. Look out for gross exaggerations of price increases.

While diamond prices have had very substantial price movement in recent years (50-60% per year), some firms would have you believe the prices rise 25% every month. Beware of outlandish claims about price movement. Don't be pushed into buying in a hurry. It's always a good time to buy diamonds, and if you miss this price increase, you'll be sure to get the next. (See **Chapter 8**)

8. Beware of short-term selling.
Diamonds are a long-term instrument. There's just no getting away from that fact. Anyone suggesting short-term profits in diamonds probably only intends to be in business for a short term. (See **Chapter 9**)

This list of deceptive practices is fairly extensive. I don't mean to scare investors away. There are many legitimate, honest diamond dealers, jewelers, and investment diamond firms. And the number is growing. But there are also many not-so-honest firms.

An investor considering any investment should proceed cautiously. There are pitfalls in every investment area, not only diamonds.

There are substantial profits to be made by investing in diamonds. I believe the future is even brighter than the past. Wise investors can reap handsome rewards if they proceed intellignetly, cautiously, and knowledgeably.

How to Evaluate Investment
Diamond Companies

Here are some of the facilities, capabilities, and services that you should look for in an investment diamond Company:

— trained gemologists
— a record of experience in the diamond industry
— a good track record in reselling stones for clients
— competitive commission rates for reselling stones (Generally these run from 7-20%)
— high marks from trade and business references (banks, Better Business Bureau, etc.)
— registration and clean record with state regulatory agencies
— provision for guarding against switching of stones, and assurance that stone and certificate match
— ability to promptly deliver top grade gemstones
— good primary sources of diamonds through good connections in the trade
— competitive pricing
— ability to inspect diamond and certificate prior to purchase

Certification
Laboratories

1. Gemological Institute of America (G.I.A.)

1660 Stewart Street
Santa Monica, CA 90404
(213) 829-2991

580 Fifth Avenue
New York, NY 10036
(212) 221-5858

606 S. Olive Street,
Suite 1122
Los Angeles, CA 90014
(213) 629-5435

2. European Gemological Laboratory (E.G.L.)

Hoveniersstraat 40
2000 Antwerp (Belgium)

608 S. Hill Street
Los Angeles, CA 90014

20 West 47th Street, Suite 300
New York, NY 10036

3. International Gemological Institute (IGI)

20 West 47th Street
New York, NY 10036

Private Vault Companies

These are private companies that have secure vaults for hire.

Safe Deposit Co. of New York
120 Broadway
New York, NY 10005

Standard Safe Deposit Co.
25 Broad Street
New York, NY 10004

Great American Silver Co.
3862 Steward Road
Doraville, GA 30340

Missouri Safe Deposit Co.
920 Walnut St.
Kansas City, MO 64106

Causey's Safe Rentals,
Inc.
1806 Layton Avenue
Fort Worth, TX67117

Wacker Drive Safe
Deposit Co.
20 N. Wacker Drive
Chicago, IL60606

The Plain Company,
Inc.
2051 Young Street
Honolulu, HI 96826

Day and Night Safe
Deposit Vaults
507 Third Avenue
Seattle,WA 98104

Banks and Trust Companies Which Accept Diamonds For Pensions Programs

American Trust Company of Hawaii, Inc.
841 Bishop Street
(808) 521-6543

Associated Administrators Ltd., Inc.
15950 Arminta Street
Van Nuys, CA 91406
(213) 997-8500

First State Bank of Oregon
1212 S.W. Sixth Avenue
P. O. Box 272
Portland, OR 97207
(503) 243-3517

Lincoln Trust Company
5600 S. Syracuse Circle
Englewood, CO 80111
(303) 771-1900

Lafayette Bank & Trust Co.
345 State Street
Bridgeport, CT 06601
(203) 367-6651

Landmark Union Trust Bank
P. O. Box 11388
St. Petersburg, FL 33733
(813) 366-8722

Richfield Bank & Trust Company
6625 Lyndale Avenue
Richfield, MN 55423
(612) 861-7355

Glossary

alluvial deposits — diamonds that are found in beds of sand or gravel along rivers or the ocean where they've been washed by water from their origins.

appraisal — the act of placing a monetary value on a diamond as opposed to giving it a quality grade.

Big Hole — a modern name for the remains of the Kimberley Mine, the first big South African mine.

"blue-white" — an old term used to describe a diamond with very little body color. Corresponds to D, E, or F color.

bort — low-grade or industrial diamonds.

bourse — an exchange, where members of the trade buy and sell diamonds.

brilliancy — the degree of a diamond's ability to reflect light internally and externally from a face-up position.

bubble — a commonly used description for a flaw or "inclusion" within a diamond.

buyer's box — a special box of various sizes in which participants at DeBeers "sights" receive their quota of rough stones.

carat — the unit of measurement (1 carat = 1/142 ounce or 200 milligrams) in which diamonds are weighed.

cape — a broad category of stones that have a yellowish tint.

Central Selling Organization (CSO) — also known as "The Syndicate" — the division of DeBeers responsible for selling rough diamonds to cutters and merchants. Based in London.

certificate — a laboratory gemologist's report attesting to a stone's color, clarity, cut grades, weight, and other qualities.

clarity grade — the degree to which a diamond is flawed.

clean — a jeweler's vague term denoting the appearance of flawlessness in a diamond.

cleavage — the crystalline planes along which diamonds can be split.

color grade — the degree to which a diamond is "white" or colorless.

crown — the facets of a diamond between the girdle and the table on a round brilliant cut diamond.

culet — the bottom point or tip of a round brilliant cut stone.

Cullinan Diamond — the largest diamond ever discovered in 1905 at the premiermine in South Africa. It was 3106 carats of gem quality, measuring 2 x 2 1/2 x 4 inches. Cut into 9 large gems, 96 smaller gems, and 9 1/2 carats of other pieces. The largest are in the British Crown Jewels.

DeKalk Farm — a farm on the Orange River in South Africa where the first South African diamond — a 21-carat stone — was discovered in 1866.

depth — the length of a diamond from table to culet relative to (in percentage terms) the stone's diameter at the girdle.

dop — a device used to hold a rough diamond during the cutting process.

E.G.L. — the European Gemological Laboratory, grades and certifies diamonds.

emerald cut — a rectangular, terraced style of cutting a diamond.

fancy — a style of diamond cut other than the popular "round brilliant;" also used to describe color diamonds (pink, blue, etc.).

feather — a feathery-looking flaw in a diamond, usually on the girdle.

fire — the dispersion of different colors from a diamond; also used to describe the brilliance of a diamond.

flaw — any imperfection on or in a diamond.

flawless — a diamond with no internal or external blemishes visible under 10-power magnification.

fluorescence — the ability of a stone to alter light as it comes in and emit different spectral colors.

gemprint — a relatively new technique of utilizing a laser beam to produce a photograph of a stone's surface characteristics for identification purposes.

G.I.A. — the Gemological Institute of America, the pathbreaking diamond grading and certification laboratory.

girdle — the widest, round edge or circumference of a diamond, at the base of the crown.

Golcanda — a city in India that was the center of the first diamond diggings.

grain — the directions of cleavage in a diamond.

Hope Diamond — a famous 45.52-carat dark blue diamond from India believed to have been cut from a larger stone. Once in the French Treasury.

HRD — Hoge Raad Voor Diamant, the Antwerp-based gemological laboratory, grades and certifies diamonds.

inclusion — an imperfection or flaw within a diamond.

industrial diamond — a diamond so discolored and imperfect that it can only be used for its hardness properties in industrial cutting and drilling.

irradiation — the process of bombarding a stone with atomic particles to enhance its color.

Kimberley — the city near which the first diamond mine in South Africa was discovered.

kimberlite pipes — the cylindrical volcanic formations in which diamonds are found.

Koh-i-noor — a 108.93-carat diamond now among the British Crown Jewels, formerly 186 carats and dating back to 14th century India.

leakage — the proclivity of a poorly cut or less than ideally cut stone not to refract to the eye the optimum amount of light. This results in a loss of brilliance.

loupe — a small magnifying glass held in the eye socket. It should be 10x (power) magnification.

melange — a mixture of diamonds of different sizes and grades.

melee — diamonds of .18-carat or less in size. Used primarily in jewelry.

Moh's scale — a simple numerical scale of hardness, with the diamond number 10, corundum 9, and so on.

Namagualand — the rich coastal diamond producing region of Southwest Africa.

Orange River — the source of much of the alluvial diamond deposits in South Africa.

pavilion — the portion of a round brilliant cut diamond between girdle and culet.

piqué — a general description for lower grade or imperfect diamonds.

point — 1/100 of a carat.

polish — the degree of smoothness of a diamond's surface.

refraction — the bending of light rays as they pass through a diamond, as opposed to reflection of light off the extended facets.

River — another archaic term for the highest (whitest) color grade. Corresponds to D, E or F.

round brilliant cut — the most popular shape and cut of stone containing 58 facets — also called Tolkowsky cut.

Russalmaz — the Soviet Union's Antwerp-based trading company engaged in the marketing of Soviet diamonds.

sawing — the separation of a rough diamond by a special saw impregnated with olive oil and diamond dust.

Scan. D.N. — the Scandanavian Diamond Nomenclature for standards of color, clarity, and cut accepted by Scandinavian countries.

scintillation — the amount of light reflection given off by a diamond viewed from different angles.

sight — the occasion where rough diamonds are bought from the DeBeers cartel every five weeks at London and other locations.

spread stone — a diamond of less than "ideal" depth, that is with a large table, small crown and wide angled pavilion.

"Syndicate" — an expression for the DeBeers cartel, especially its Central Selling Organization, which controls the marketing of rough stones.

table — the top facet of the diamond when viewed from above, octagonal in shape.

Tolkowsky Cut — the original style and proportions of the round brilliant stone designed by the mathematician Marcel Tolkowsky in 1919; designed to yield a stone's maximum amount of light.

twinning lines — visible lines within a diamond showing the planes between crystals.

VVS — "very, very small inclusions", the first category below "Flawless" when grading the clarity of a diamond. (VS is "very small").

Wesselton — a term in the old River-to-light yellow system used to refer to stones with only slight color.

zircon — a simulated diamond with different characteristics but superficial likeness.

Index

Index